"Tony is a master at helping leaders understand how to optimize the performance of their teams, and in so doing become effective followers. *Beyond the Leader* is a fantastic guide for all leaders to realize that potential."

—Brad Adams
President & CEO, Southwest Transplant Alliance

"In my many years of trying to learn and practice effective *leadership* the 7 Disciplines that Define Extraordinary Teams have impacted me the most. I've never seen the relationship between engagement and execution depicted so clearly, and I find myself actively thinking about this daily, both personally and professionally."

—Kim Burak
Chief People Officer, CityVet

"Being a leader isn't really about holding a title or running an organization. It's a mindset, a way of thinking. In *Beyond the Leader* the mindset every leader needs is embodied in the 7 disciplines. Leaders who learn these disciplines and use them with their teams will soon see the power of the follower come alive. That is the essential mindset all leaders need to know and use to be truly successful."

—Michael Williams
DO, MD, Chancellor, The University of North Texas System

"*Beyond the Leader* is another fantastic building block in Tony's mission to make dynamic and healthy workplace cultures accessible. I found each of the 7 Disciplines is approachable and instantly actionable for teams large and small."

—Lindsay Wilson
President, Corgan

"In a world where we're all moving so fast, Dr. Bridwell's ability to communicate succinctly and clearly has never been more important. His concepts are simple, but highly effective helping our leadership team connect the dots and achieve superior results. He is the real deal."

—Dean Setoguchi
President and CEO, Keyera

"Dr. Tony Bridwell has done it again!!! What happens when we're not there? Have we as leaders provided the tools, clarity, space, trust, energy, and vision for a team to test, learn, adapt, lean in, and execute? Are we celebrating the wins and allowing space to recharge and reconnect when needed? *Beyond the Leader* guides the reader along an actionable journey to create and build impactful teams and healthy organizations."

—Jason McCann
CEO, VARI

"In *Beyond the Leader*, Dr. Tony Bridwell masterfully challenges the myth of the lone hero and invites us into a powerful new narrative – one where high performing teams are built and connected on shared purpose, mutual accountability, and collective strength. Through an engaging fable and the seven disciplines that shape extraordinary teams, Bridwell continues to redefine what it means to lead – and to follow. This is a must-read for anyone committed to building optimized, people-first organizations."

—John Luke Spitler
CEO, The Encompass Group

BEYOND THE
LEADER

BEYOND THE
LEADER

A Fable
about the
7 Disciplines
that define
**Extraordinary
Teams**

TONY A. BRIDWELL, EdD

WILEY

Published by John Wiley & Sons, Inc., Hoboken, New Jersey.
Published simultaneously in Canada.

The manufacturer's authorized representative according to the EU General Product Safety Regulation is Wiley-VCH GmbH, Boschstr. 12, 69469 Weinheim, Germany, e-mail: Product_Safety@wiley.com.

Limit of Liability/Disclaimer of Warranty: While the publisher and author have used their best efforts in preparing this book, they make no representations or warranties with respect to the accuracy or completeness of the contents of this book and specifically disclaim any implied warranties of merchantability or fitness for a particular purpose. No warranty may be created or extended by sales representatives or written sales materials. The advice and strategies contained herein may not be suitable for your situation. You should consult with a professional where appropriate. Further, readers should be aware that websites listed in this work may have changed or disappeared between when this work was written and when it is read. Neither the publisher nor authors shall be liable for any loss of profit or any other commercial damages, including but not limited to special, incidental, consequential, or other damages.

For general information on our other products and services or for technical support, please contact our Customer Care Department within the United States at (800) 762-2974, outside the United States at (317) 572-3993 or fax (317) 572-4002.

Wiley also publishes its books in a variety of electronic formats. Some content that appears in print may not be available in electronic formats. For more information about Wiley products, visit our web site at www.wiley.com.

Library of Congress Cataloging-in-Publication Data is Available:

ISBN 9781394364558 (cloth)
ISBN 9781394364565 (ePub)
ISBN 9781394364572 (ePDF)

Cover Design: Paul McCarthy
Cover Art: © Getty Images | Shuoshu

Printed and bound by CPI Group (UK) Ltd, Croydon, CR0 4YY

C9781394364558_310725

The journey of learning reshapes not just what we know but who we become – one reflection, one decision, one act at a time.

Contents

Acknowledgments   *xiii*
About the Author   *xvii*

Introduction   **1**

1 The Prologue   **5**
The Note   8
The Words   11
The Lecture   16
The 7 Disciplines   22

2 The Learning Discipline   **27**
Redefining Leadership and Followership   30
The Starting Point   32
The Barriers to the Learning Discipline   36
Thomas's Breakthrough   37
Thomas's Journal Recap   39
        Learning Discipline: Lessons from Leah   39

3 The Clarity Discipline   **43**
What Is Clarity Discipline?   44
Why Teams Struggle with Clarity   47
How to Achieve Clarity   48

Clarity in Action 50

Leah's Wisdom 53

Thomas's Journal Recap 53

    Clarity Discipline: Lessons from Leah 53

4 The Safety Discipline 57

Safety: The Air We Breathe 60

The Four Seeds of Trust 62

Overcoming Weeds in the Garden 64

Recognizing and Addressing Weeds 66

The Role of Faith in Trust 67

Thomas's Journal Recap 68

    Safety Discipline: Lessons from Leah 68

5 The Connection Discipline 71

What Is Connection Discipline? 73

    Collaborators: The Team 74

    Coaches: The Guides 80

    Counselors: The Unpackers 83

Building Connections 92

Thomas's Journal Recap 94

    Connection Discipline:
    Lessons from Leah 94

6 The Action Discipline 97

The Foundation of Execution 98

Decisive Decisions 99

The Polarity Paradox 100

Both/And Thinking 103

Engaging the Team 105

Avoiding the Priority Trap 106
Understanding the Trap 106
Applying It 109
    The Power of Both/And 110
    Aligned Execution 110
    Sustained Momentum 111
Thomas's Journal Recap 112
    Action Discipline: Lessons from Leah 112

7 The Adaptability Discipline 115
Situational Awareness 115
Feedback Loops 115
Strategic Flexibility 116
Thomas's Journal Recap 118
    Adaptability Discipline:
    Lessons from Leah 118

8 The Celebration Discipline 121
Acknowledgment 121
Reflection 121
Renewal 122
Execution in Action 122
Thomas's Journal Recap 123
    Celebration Discipline:
    Lessons from Leah 123

9 The Final Word 125
Leah's Insights on Trust and Faith 126
The Doubt Inside 127

The Disciplines Revisited: Trust and
Faith in Focus   131
    Learning Discipline: Start by Listening   131
    Clarity Discipline: Align Expectations   131
    Safety Discipline: Building with Faith,
    Vulnerability, and Trust   132
    Connection Discipline: Create
    Shared Moments   133
    Action Discipline: Making Decisive
    Decisions   134
    Adaptability Discipline: The Ability
    to Check and Adjust   136
    The Letter   138
    The Celebration Discipline:
    Telling the Story   139

Appendix: Resource Material   *143*
Index   *149*

Acknowledgments

After writing seven acknowledgment pages for my previous books, I find myself in the unique position of having a new publisher. What a great privilege and honor it is to be included on the Wiley team of authors.

That said, with a new publisher comes a new team of professional literary nerds, such as me, whose passion for the books they publish rivals mine at times. Let it be known that these people love what they do.

The Wiley team is headed by Shannon Vargo, whose travel schedule may give mine a run for the money. It should be noted that my good friend and now fellow Wiley author, Ben Utecht, introduced Shannon to me in the fall of 2024.

It is a blessing that Shannon had the vision and saw potential in my work, which ultimately brought me to type these words. While her name undoubtedly appears in the acknowledgment section of hundreds of books, I am most grateful for her appearance in this book.

Additionally, a team of three editors has been assigned to this project. I am assured that it is not because I am higher maintenance than other authors but because it is just how they take care of their authors. For now, I choose to believe that.

Alison Bohn heads the editorial team. Alison gets me! Her gentle spirit, that of a saint, comes to life with a fiery passion when she talks about books. I am grateful for her drive to produce a game-changer book.

Purvi Patel, the managing editor, keeps the trains running through production with Swiss-like precision. Kim Wimpsett, my developmental editor, is the red-pen editor who keeps the story moving in the right direction. Thank you for your patience and professionalism as you guided me through the Wiley process.

Back home, a team also supports the efforts of producing a book. My work team at The Encompass Group has been instrumental in supporting this project in too many ways to list. My long-time friend and now boss, John Luke Spitler, is the engine that drives The Encompass Group to be a leader in people and technology optimization. His friendship and encouragement have set an example for me, and I am forever grateful. Additionally, my constant thought partner, Robert Rich, is a force to be reckoned with. His insights and critical thinking regarding teams have been invaluable.

The downside of writing an acknowledgment page is that once you start listing the names of all the people who have supported you over the journey of writing and producing a book, you are almost sure to leave people out. Not on purpose, but because of the sheer number of individuals that come into your orbit during the process, all of whom play some type of important role. People who have read early versions of the manuscript or clients who participated in workshop sessions as we unpacked the core model of the 7 Disciplines, and those who offered feedback on all the various aspects of the process, from the cover design to the interior layout. To all of those people, thank you!

The one group not to be left out is my family. When I look at my family as a team, the 7 Disciplines have come to life over the last decade as this group of amazing people, with their long-suffering patience with me, as I have learned how to be a better follower to become a better leader. It is a given that I still have work to do but with their support anything in possible. They are truly extraordinary.

About the Author

Dr. Tony Bridwell is an organizational behaviorist with 25-plus years of experience working with global organizations related to employee experience and culture. As Chief Talent Officer for The Encompass Group, a people and technology optimization company, he leads the firm's organizational consulting practice and serves as Practice Leader of the E3 Leadership Academy.

Most recently Dr. Bridwell led the award-winning People Group function of the global tax and technology firm Ryan, LLC as their Chief People Officer. Before his role at Ryan, he was the Chief People Officer for Brinker International and a Senior Partner with the global culture consultancy, Culture Partners.

Tony is an accomplished author of seven books, an international speaker, having presented in 44 countries, and is a sought-after consultant and advisor specializing in leadership, followership, and culture. Dr. Bridwell was selected as the 2015 HR Executive of the Year by Dallas HR (the local SHRM affiliate), won the 2015 Strategic Leadership Award from Strategic Excellence HR, and was most recently recognized as a 2022 top 50 HR Professional by OnCon Icon Awards.

Dr. Bridwell's academic journey is as diverse as his professional one, with studies in architecture, theology, and business culminating in a Bachelor of Science in Business, a Master of Business Administration (MBA) degree, and a Doctorate in Organizational Intelligence where his research focused on leadership and followership. His commitment to education extends to his role as an adjunct professor at Trevecca Nazarene University in Nashville and SMU in Dallas, where he teaches MBA students Executive Leadership.

Beyond academia, he is deeply involved in various organizations, including the Society for Human Resource Management (SHRM) and the board of directors for Southwest Transplant Alliance. His personal commitment to organ donation, as a living organ donor, is a testament to his belief in the power of purpose and the potential to save lives through organ and tissue donation and transplantation.

About the Author

Introduction

It has been said, although the origin of the phrase is still a mystery, *the art of writing is knowing when to stop*. Hemingway is reported as saying, "It is best to stop when you are going good and know what will happen next." For some, the challenge is writing the first word; for others, it's knowing when to lay down the pen. Such is the delicate balance every writer must achieve.

This book is the fourth in a series that began five years ago with *Saturday Morning Tea*. Readers who have been with the series since that first installment will find some familiarity with the opening scene, as I deliberately intertwined the stories. There is no need to worry if this is the first book you encounter in this series. Welcome to the journey. Each book in the series has been a standalone read but with a simple thread of continuity woven within and developing through each book to present a far richer read, having read the series from beginning to end.

The Follower Effect, the predecessor to this book, was the product of more than three years of research related to my doctoral studies. That work dug deeply into what happens at the intersection of leadership and followership, with a strong focus on how the duality of leadership and followership shapes individuals and organizational culture. While *The Follower Effect* captured the heart of that research, this book examines insights that, if I may paraphrase Hemingway's wisdom, *I knew were ready but best saved for what came next*. It is time to look beyond the leader to find the true essence of an extraordinary team.

That said, let's unpack the idea of a team. While many teams seek the basics of operating in an effective manner – achieving the desired outcomes on time – an extraordinary team is optimized taking performance to a higher level. Teams have two halves, they need to be engaged and execute. When teams are engaged but lack execution, they are energized but struggle to deliver desirable outcomes. When teams execute, but are not engaged, there is also a cost to consider, the cost toward the people. It is teams that are engaged and execute that are extraordinary as they have optimized how they deliver outcomes, creating a flywheel effect of continuous learning and improvement in the process.

As noted in the title of the book, there are seven disciplines we have discovered that, when operating as a system, help to ensure a team is engaged, and can execute, or said another way, become optimized.

The key to bringing these two halves together and holding it in place is the connection, which is anchored in individuals who understand their role as both a leader and follower. This book explores how these seven disciplines empower teams to move beyond mere effectiveness, unlocking their full potential through reflection, alignment, and growth.

When we started the journey, we met Leah, a young, first-time manager who was introduced in *Saturday Morning Tea*. Her life-changing relationship with the unlikely mentor, *The Professor*, set the stage for a decades-long journey of growth and discovery. As Leah's story unfolds across the series, she evolves from first-time manager to seasoned leader and ultimately steps into the role of The Professor herself. In each book, we continue to meet new characters that show us lessons to carry on in life and continue the idea that life has its seasons for learning, leading, and growing.

While this book is about teams and is meant to resonate deeply with people who lead or work with teams, its lessons certainly extend well beyond the workplace. The disciplines explored here, *learning, clarity, safety, connection, action, adaptability,* and *celebration,* apply equally to our family lives, volunteer efforts, classrooms, and communities. Teams are not confined to office walls; they exist wherever individuals come together to achieve a shared purpose.

The more I research the duality between followership and leadership, the more fascinated I become with how effective followership drives team optimization. It's a fresh and necessary nuance in team dynamics, an essential next step in how we develop and manage teams. When we understand and embrace the interplay between followership and leadership, we unlock the potential for teams to operate at their highest level.

While this book, like my other seven, is a leadership fable and thus fictional, it is research-based. Therefore, while the ideas, concepts, and insights are research-driven, they are not cited in traditional APA formatting to avoid distracting from the story. That said, the appendix contains a list of references used to construct the story.

So here we are again, joining our heroine Leah once more as she imparts the lessons of the seven disciplines that define extraordinary teams. Through her story, we'll explore how these disciplines can transform how teams function and how individuals show up as followers and leaders to something greater than themselves. Welcome to the journey.

The bespectacled, ruddy-faced young man sat staring at the blinking cursor on the screen. He desperately searched for the right words as his fingers remained frozen over the keyboard. Deep in thought, he reached to take a sip of his steaming cup of tea.

"Hot!" he exclaimed impatiently, dropping the cup back into the saucer. "Figures," he grumbled as he turned back toward his screen.

The small café has seen many businesses in its century-plus of existence. Still, it has enjoyed the last 40 years as the area's eclectic go-to spot for freshly roasted coffee or unique blends of tea paired perfectly with freshly baked pastries. Depending on who you ask, the pastries bring people back more than the coffee or tea.

The exposed brick wall framed the far end of the café, and a half-dozen small tables and mismatched chairs filled the space in front of the serving bar. The brass bell attached to the antique wood and glass door announced each customer with a familiar, calming sound.

Moments after a ring of the bell, the young man was greeted unexpectedly. "Writing a story?" a delicate voice spoke from above him. Looking up, the young man's eyes met the kind smile of the sun-drenched figure speaking to him. Short-cropped, silver hair perfectly framed the face of the distinguished lady who carefully balanced her blueberry scone in one hand and her cup of hot tea in the other.

"I once knew a writer and storyteller who sat in this same spot," she said as she sat down across the communal table. "What story are you trying to write?" she asked, sipping her tea with care.

Curious, the young man surveyed her and then slumped back into the antique chair. He let out a heavy sigh of defeat. "An email to the girl I love," he said as his voice trailed off in resignation.

"Ah, matters of the heart," she smiled mischievously. "Now, that is a noble story to tell. But why the long face?"

His extended pause allowed the distinguished lady to sample the warm blueberry scone and take another satisfying sip of her tea.

"She doesn't know how I feel," the young man softly replied. "I feel like this whole relationship will crumble if this email is not perfect."

The lady placed her scone on her plate and shifted her weight slightly in her chair to make eye contact with the young man. "I've learned in life that in work, play, or relationships, we are designed to connect with others. How we do that determines how well we do this thing called life."

The young man gently nodded his head as he hung on every word.

"Would you like some help?" she asked in a tender tone. The young man's eyes brightened with a combination of suspicion and hope.

"How can you help me?"

The lady smiled gently as she pulled out a notebook and fountain pen. "My name is Leah. Let me tell you a story…."

The Note

Leah opened her well-worn notebook to a blank page to record insights from the young man. It seemed as if it was only yesterday, and the roles were reversed as Leah, a then-young manager, sat in the café, desperately looking for the words to write in an email. Then, all those years ago, Leah met her mentor, whom everyone on campus called The Professor.

Years later, after a successful career culminating as the CEO of a global company, Leah decided to return to campus and become a professor in the business school. Once word was out that Leah was teaching, her classes became the most popular on campus, with students from non-business majors taking her class for the practical lessons on life.

"Thank you, Leah. I'm Thomas." The young man offered as he shifted in his chair.

"Thomas, tell me why this note is so important to you." Leah began cradling the pen in her hand, ready to record Thomas's thoughts. The notebook, one of many, contained her most recent notes from various conversations. Earlier in her life, she was purely digital in her note-taking, but she still enjoys tapping on her laptop or tablet's keys from time to time.

Her mentor, the Professor, shared the value of putting pen to paper.

Thomas slowly dropped the screen on his laptop to remove the barrier between him and Leah as he prepared his thoughts. "Maya and I met two years ago during our second-year internship at a Wall Street investment firm. The pace was grueling, with little time for ourselves, but with what time we had, Maya and I spent it together exploring the city. Both of us were from small towns in the South and spent very little time in New York until college," Thomas recalled as his face lit up thinking about Maya.

"Relationships developed in the trenches have powerful bonds," Leah said as she recorded a thought in her journal. "What happened at the end of your internship?" Leah asked as she continued with her scone.

"Maya accepted a job with the New York investment bank, and I took a job with a financial service company in Dallas on a service delivery team," Thomas said with mixed emotions in his voice.

Leah's gentle gaze prompted Thomas to continue his story. "For the last 18 months, Maya and I have been making it work long-distance." Thomas continued

with a slight increase in intensity in his voice. "But…"
He began as his voice trailed off.

"You feel as if you are growing apart?" Leah offered,
finishing Thomas's thought. Without making eye contact, Thomas nodded as he picked up his tea to take
a drink.

"I see." Leah offered in a comforting tone. "You feel
as if you are losing your connection with each other."
She began. "Tell me, Thomas. Do you believe this is
because you are in separate cities?" Leah asked in her
professorial voice.

Thomas looked up from his tea with an increased
curiosity based on the question. "We talk almost every
day," Thomas said with confidence.

"Yet, you feel less connected?" Leah offered. "Why
do you think that is?" Leah continued. Thomas sat
motionless for several seconds as he contemplated
the question.

After taking a bite of scone, Leah offered, "Thomas,
there is a difference between talking and communicat-
ing. Connections are strengthened in the communication between people." Leah added, taking a sip of her
tea. "Have you ever had a conversation where you're

saying everything but feeling like you're saying nothing at all?" she asked, a hint of a smile playing at her lips.

Thomas nodded, recognizing the familiar feeling.

"Real connection," Leah continued, "isn't in our words. It's in the feeling we leave behind based on the tone and emotion of those words."

Thomas thought of his last call with Maya, the way her voice had softened when she talked about her day. He'd responded, but maybe he hadn't really *heard* her.

"Let's work on that note," Leah said as she placed her tea gently in the saucer and picked up her pen.

The Words

Fall filled the air with the brilliance of color and crisp, cool temperatures, making the campus brimming with energy. The century-old campus was a living story of past, present, and future. The Georgian architecture framed the campus in a Norman Rockwall-like picture lost on most of the students as they rambled across campus, evading the small autonomous robots delivering takeout meals to students at all points of the sprawling city campus.

Leah was strolling through the quadrangle on her way to class when an energetic person approached, waving his hand.

"Professor!" exclaimed the young man.

Instantly, Leah began reviewing all the students in her mind to recall the name of the person quickly approaching. As one of the newest members of the faculty, Leah had a full teaching load. After over 20 years in the corporate marketplace, over half as CEO of a multi-national publicly traded company, it was time to move into a new season of life where she could share her wealth of knowledge with future generations. Admittedly, the idea of teaching was not a stretch given her longtime mentor, a professor she met when she was a first-time manager. Those moments together forever made a significant impact on her life. Now, it was her season to give back.

Leah's face broke into a broad smile within moments, realizing the young man was not a student but Thomas from the café. "Hello, Thomas." Leah began. "It's so nice to see you. What brings you to campus?"

A bit out of breath, Thomas began. "I was hoping to find you and thank you for your help with my note to Maya."

"And how is Maya?" Leah asked, still smiling.

"Amazing! She wanted me to tell you thank you." Thomas said, beaming with satisfaction. "But that is only partly of why I am here." He continued.

Leah's face expressed her curiosity as Thomas continued. "Maya suggested I ask your opinion about an issue I am having at work with my team." Thomas continued with a hint of eagerness in his voice.

"Well, you must walk with me to tell me more about your team," Leah said as she motioned Thomas toward her next class.

Thomas's face lit up with excitement as the two headed toward the three-story business school building surrounding the quadrangle. For over a century, the rooms within these walls have housed some of the brightest minds in the world, providing the space to equip them to become difference-makers on the world stage of business. The steps leading to the oversized double door were crowded with students and faculty navigating between classes. Only a few years had passed since Thomas had completed his undergrad studies, so he blended in well among the students.

Arriving at the lecture hall a few minutes early, Leah made her way toward the front of the room to plug in her lecture materials. As she descended the gentle steps of the room, she was greeted by the students who had arrived early to acquire a good seat. Thomas followed, in tow, as the two arrived at the lectern.

"Tell me about your team, Thomas." Leah began as she reached into her bag to extract a USB drive to insert into the podium.

"My boss, the VP of Operations, assembled a cross-functional team of five people to work on Project Leprechaun," Thomas said, his voice trailing off, and he announced the team's name aloud.

Leah paused and looked up at Thomas, noting the tone change in his words. "I sense a story coming," Leah said with a comforting smile. Thomas's face crinkled as he searched for the right words.

"Well, you see, Project Leprechaun has been tasked with finding a way to breathe growth into our cornerstone product line, Plexon. For 25 years, Plexon has dominated the marketplace with little competition. Now, the company is producing new innovative offerings that are growing like crazy, but Plexon has started to slow in sales. So, our team is tasked with finding ways to bring Plexon back to growth," Thomas explained

"Sounds exciting." Leah offered as she picked up the clicker to advance to her first slide. Thomas's head dipped in a bit of embarrassment. "I am guessing the team doesn't see it that way?" Leah continued noticing Thomas's response.

"The team feels a bit like, well, you know, in PE class when teams are picked to play kickball and you are the last to be picked for a team. It feels a bit like that." Thomas offered as he fidgeted with his hands as he talked.

Leah smiled as she tried to comfort Thomas. "There is much to unpack there, Thomas. Some of which are hidden within your kickball metaphor. But we will save that for another discussion." Leah offered. "For now, if you have time, I think you will enjoy our class topic today." She said as she pointed to the oversized screen behind her.

Thomas looked up for the first time to see the words on the ink-black backdrop: "The Follower Effect: The Story of an Optimized Team."

With an expression generally reserved for your first trip to Disney, Thomas began to shake his head in disbelief.

"Well, it's been a hot minute since I sat in a lecture hall, but it seems today has been pre-destined." He said as he made his way to the only open seat in the front row.

The Lecture

As Leah began her lecture, Thomas dug into his backpack and produced a laptop. Quickly, he set up shop, blending in with the other students as they diligently recorded notes from the professor's talk. The first slide to be revealed generated a flurry of typing as students quickly saw the value of the quote before them.

"Each of us is wonderfully and beautifully made, designed to interpret our life experiences through the lens of story," Leah began as the students furiously typed to keep up with her words. "It's how we understand the world, pass along wisdom, and make sense of life's complexity. From ancient oral tradition to modern film, stories shape our sense of identity and inform our behaviors more than we realize," she continued.

"But among all the story arcs that have defined human storytelling, one has had a more significant impact upon our minds than any other: the Hero's Journey,"

Leah noted as she deliberately made her way toward the front row of the cascading auditorium. "First introduced by a professor in Columbia University, Joseph Campbell, who in 1949, after years of studying myths across multiple cultures, identified a pattern, known as a monomyth. His book, *The Hero with a Thousand Faces* changed how we view storytelling," Leah continued as the tone of her voice added a sense of personal connection to story.

"This narrative – where a single hero ventures forth, meets challenges, and returns transformed – has been in our cultural DNA. It's the foundation for myth, literature, and even leadership theory. It has fueled some of our best stories, from *Star Wars* to *The Lord of the Rings*," she said as several students raised their heads with the mention of two of the all-time great movie franchises.

"And." Leah continued, "although the hero's journey is valuable, it can create challenges when applied to teams." "Why?" She said pausing for effect. "It tends to be centered around a single person, the hero."

"One person standing alone. One being meant to be apart from everyone else. It can create the perception that leadership means stepping forward alone to be a hero."

"And in my view," Leah began, "that's a problem. Not because the Hero's Journey isn't correct, but because it's incomplete."

"Nobody succeeds in real life alone. The world doesn't thrive due to solo heroes – it thrives because of teams, communities, and interdependent efforts. The best heroes in storytelling don't succeed without mentors, friends, and those who stand by them. And yet, our leadership paradigms have too often focused on the leader as the central figure in the story, at times neglecting to recognize that the leader, at times, must also become a follower," She added in a confident tone.

"Here's where followership comes into play," she said.

"In teams, organizations, and workplaces, great leaders aren't those who try to be the hero in every situation but those who recognize the power of followership – in themselves and in those around them. Real leadership isn't about being a soloist; it's about generating a dynamic in which leadership and followership blend and shift as circumstances dictate," Leah said moving her hands to draw an infinity loop in mid-air.

"But even so, followership has a bad reputation. It's often confused with passivity or submission when, in reality, it's the driving force behind every high-performing team. Followership is what enables teams to achieve their highest potential, moving them beyond mere effectiveness to something greater," she continued.

"With that in mind, let's explore a new leadership approach – one that doesn't rely on a single hero but rather on the collective strength of the group. Because if we want to build truly optimized teams, we have to move beyond the leader," Leah offered as pointed the clicker toward her laptop, advancing the slide

"Leadership and Followership Are Two-Sides of the Same Coin." The slide read. "We often confuse leadership and followership as being separate constructs." Leah began. Her presence in the room was commanding as she slowly paced the front of the room, out from behind the podium, where many professors tend to linger. "We must keep in mind that we are constantly cycling in and out of our roles as leader and follower throughout the day." Leah continued. "It is in fact that we are both and should pay close attention to as we navigate life," she added reassuringly.

Leah paused, letting her words settle before moving to the next slide. "Think of leadership and followership as a constant dance," she said, her gaze sweeping across the room. "Every team, every relationship, and every project require us to shift fluidly between these roles. When we lead well, we are informed by our experiences as followers; when we follow well, we influence and shape our own leadership and the leaders around us." She noticed Thomas leaning forward, his eyes locked on the screen, absorbing every word. "This isn't about titles or positions. It's about understanding that the strength of followership enhances leadership, and followership is strengthened by the lessons learned from leadership."

She clicked to reveal a new slide, a single quote highlighted on a deep black background: *"Learning and Accountability is the Bridge Between Follower and Leader."* Leah let the words resonate as she spoke. "In your roles as followers, you each hold the power to create change by owning your impact while committing to continuous learning. Accountability is not just for the person at the top. True accountability and true growth begin with each of us, as followers, committing to bring our best to the table – through reflecting, rethinking, and acting, without waiting for someone else to take the first step." She noticed several students nodding, and Thomas's look of recognition told her that the message was hitting close to home. "When we each take ownership of our learning and our impact," she continued, "the by-product is stronger teams, evidenced by high levels of psychological safety, innovative thinking, and delivered excellence."

Leah continued, letting the message of shared account-ability settle across the room. "Effective followership," she said, "is a form of shared leadership. It's about modeling standards for others through your stories, leveraging your influence with a modest demand for recognition or authority. And when teams embrace this, they move from a group of individuals to a cohesive unit that drives results."

Thomas was riveted, his thoughts spiraling back to Project Leprechaun. Could this continuous learning, shared accountability concept transform how his team viewed their role in the company? By collectively taking ownership, they could become the spark that reignited Plexon's growth instead of feeling like the last picked for kickball. He'd seen how small changes in mindset could shift relationships, like with Maya – maybe it could also shift the dynamics on his team.

Leah transitioned to a discussion exercise. "Turn to the person beside you," she instructed, "and discuss a moment when you felt empowered when in follower mode to influence a project or decision." Thomas turned to his neighbor, a bright-eyed undergrad who seemed eager to engage.

After exchanging stories for a few moments, Thomas felt a renewed sense of purpose. Leah's words on learning, accountability, and followership gave him a new perspective on Project Leprechaun and his role within the team. As the exercise concluded, Leah brought the class back to attention.

"Remember," she said, "teams thrive not on individuals waiting to be led but on individuals willing to lead and follow, regardless of their position. It's when every member engages in a learning mindset and steps up with shared accountability that real transformation happens."

The 7 Disciplines

After the class was dismissed, the usual rush of students with additional questions made their way to the front of the lecture hall. Thomas silently closed the lid of his laptop while digesting the last 55 minutes. His mind quickly connected with his team and how they have struggled to gel and make progress.

Amid the clamor of the room, Leah's voice made its way to Thomas. "Want to walk with me?" Leah asked. Thomas looked up with a smile that answered the question without words.

Thomas contemplated his next question as the two entered the crowded corridor. Before he could speak, Leah broke the silence.

"You might be wondering, what now?" Leah began as Thomas nodded. "If you are willing to invest the time, we could talk more about what makes a team work at its highest potential, beyond being just effective but fully optimized," Leah began.

Thomas paused as he fully grasped the moment. "Truthfully, I was just hoping to be effective and deliver our objective," Thomas said with a hint of defeated humility in his voice.

Leah's smile offered Thomas a sense of compassion and safety. Her thoughts raced back to a time when she faced a similar crisis.

"Be encouraged, Thomas," Leah began. "Being effective is part of the journey. However, if not optimized, a team can appear to be effective by delivering results, only to have team members burn out or plateau over time, and even experience declining performance," Leah continued.

Coming to the building's rotunda, the three-story space was filled with clusters of tables and chairs occupied by students with laptops in hand. The voluminous space was bright, with natural light streaming in from the multistory leaded windows.

The Prologue

Leah stopped. It was apparent that Thomas had more questions than Leah had time for in her packed schedule.

"Thomas, we can connect later this week. Until then, I have some homework for you if you are up for an assignment," she asked with a slight grin. Thomas nodded as he retrieved his phone to take notes.

"Excellent," Leah exclaimed. "Optimized teams master seven disciplines: *learning, clarity, trust, connection, action, adaptation,* and *celebration.* Each discipline serves a distinct purpose, and great teams know how to shift between them seamlessly." She continued. "As teams navigate their challenges, they cycle through different modes or disciplines of focus. These seven disciplines are like gears; optimized teams know how to shift seamlessly between them. Today's lecture was foundational to activating these disciplines."

"Thomas," Leah began, "Each discipline has a purpose, and the magic happens when teams learn to shift fluidly between them."

Thomas typed furiously into his phone, his mind already racing with connections to his team.

"Your first assignment," Leah continued, "is to ask your team how they define leadership and followership.

Understanding their perspectives will help you see where your team stands – and where you might need to grow."

She adjusted her bag on her shoulder and began ascending the marble staircase steps. "When you're ready, meet me on Saturday morning. I enjoy a cup of tea early Saturday before the day gets going. We'll talk about how to start applying these disciplines to your team."

Thomas smiled, a renewed sense of purpose lighting up his face. "Thank you, Leah. I'll be there."

As he made his way out of the building, he thought about his team on Project Leprechaun. Perhaps, he realized, they weren't as stuck as they seemed.

Chapter 2

The Learning Discipline

Thomas spotted Leah at a café table by the window. The little shop had a distinct English vibe with deep gray-blue paneled walls and a painted ceiling adorned with antique chandeliers. The room's center framed the marble fireplace with two identical hunter-green tufted couches deep enough to get lost for an extended period of time. While the aroma filling the air was that of the finest freshly roasted coffee, ground and prepared to perfection with each cup, this café was known for its premium loose-leaf tea selection and service, one of only a few in the city.

As the server approached their table, it was immediately apparent that professionalism and kindness were deeply ingrained in the small café's ethos. Her long hair was pulled perfectly into a tight ponytail, allowing her bright smile and intentional eye contact to tell a story of care before any words were spoken. "It is wonderful to see you, Professor, "came the morning greeting. Shall I bring you the usual this morning?" she continued.

"Yes, Jaymi. That would be wonderful." Leah replied with the level of comfort of two old friends having a conversation.

"And for your guest this morning?" Jaymi continued.

Leah glanced at Thomas, who had hung his bag over the chair and made himself comfortable. Still clearing the cobwebs from his brain, Thomas exclaimed, "Caffeine, please."

Leah glanced at Jaymi and said with a wink, "Bring a service for two and a blueberry scone for me and for Thomas, please."

In moments, Jaymi reappeared with a service tray presentation balanced by one hand, adorned with a brass teapot, porcelain cups and saucers, and two warm lemon and blueberry scones, many would argue, the best in the city. Jaymi arranged the tea service on a gold-adorned placemat with effortless precision before Leah and Thomas.

Leah lifted to pour from the polished brass teapot before her, steam curling gently from the spout. As Leah flipped the tea timer, she glanced up as Thomas took in the entire presentation, her calm demeanor somehow steadying the chaotic swirl of thoughts in his head.

The café hummed with activity: the soft clinking of dishes, the low hum of conversations, and the hissing of the milk steamer at the bar as baristas drizzled the flawless leaf design into the waiting brew. Leah poured herself a cup of London Baker Special tea, her movements slow and deliberate, like someone who had mastered the art of patience.

"Enjoy, Thomas," she said, handing him the cup and saucer of freshly poured tea. "How was the assignment?"

Thomas gently settled into the black ladder-back chair while simultaneously extracting a well-worn journal from his bag. He dug around a side pocket in his backpack, looking for his favorite pen as he began.

"Let's just say it was, well, enlightening. As you said, I asked my group how they define leadership and followership. Most of them think leaders are the ones calling the shots, and followers are, well, sheep."

Leah chuckled softly, placing her cup on the table. "And what about you? Do you agree with their assessment?"

Thomas fidgeted with his pen and journal. "I mean, I used to think that way. Leaders lead, followers follow – it sounded pretty simple. But after reading their responses and thinking about it, I'm unsure anymore. Some of the best ideas on my team have come from people stepping up when I least expected it."

Leah nodded, looking quite pleased. "That realization, Thomas, is where learning begins, when we start questioning long-held assumptions. Leadership and followership aren't opposites. As we discussed in class, they're complementary roles, and the best teams know how to navigate the space between them."

Redefining Leadership and Followership

Leah leaned forward, her voice steady but firm. "Let's break it down. Most people think of leaders as the ones giving orders, making decisions, and taking responsibility for the team. But real leadership isn't about being in charge; it's about being accountable, internally first, then externally. It's about creating an environment where others can thrive."

Thomas scribbled furiously in his notebook. "So, leaders aren't necessarily the ones in the spotlight?"

"That depends," Leah said, taking another sip of tea. "There is a great deal of focus put on leaders. Some of that focus is necessary given the role. However, there are times when being the leader is most definitely not about being in the spotlight," she continued.

"That brings us to the idea of followership. Here's where most people get it wrong. They think followers are passive or unquestioning. But effective followership is anything but docile; it's dynamic and proactive."

She gestured toward the room around them. "Great followers ask questions, challenge assumptions, and hold leaders to a higher level of thinking. They're actively engaged, bringing their unique perspectives and strengths to the table. We would say they are independent critical thinkers," Leah added.

Thomas nodded slowly. "So, followership is about contributing, not just doing what you're told?"

Leah smiled. "You've got it. The best leaders are also great followers. They know when to listen, when to support, and when to let someone else step up. **Effective followers are focused on the mission of the team and organization while also being active partners in delivering results.** Leadership and followership are dynamic roles, and everyone on the team moves between them depending on the situation."

The Starting Point

Thomas closed his journal, leaning back in his chair. "Okay, I'm seeing how this ties back to the assignment. But where does *Learning Discipline* fit into all of this?"

Leah set her teacup down, folding her hands on the table. "You mentioned that your team has struggled. I'm curious, when was the last time they stopped to consider why they're struggling," Leah asked.

Thomas frowned. "I'm not sure we have ever done that."

Leah smiled, "That's the first step. The *Learning Discipline* is where it all begins. It's the foundation for every other discipline because it's where we *reflect, rethink,* and *grow.* It's about creating space for curiosity, both as a leader and as a follower."

She gestured toward Thomas's notebook. "Think about the responses you got from your team. What did they tell you about how your team sees these roles?"

Thomas flipped through his phone for his notes from the team, his brow furrowed. "They think leadership means taking all the responsibility, and followership means just doing what you're told. Honestly, I've probably reinforced that idea without meaning to. I've been so focused on leading that I've forgotten to listen or let anyone else take the lead."

Leah poured another cup of tea for herself and watched as Thomas flipped through his journal. "You've received meaningful feedback from your team, Thomas," she said. "But the real value of learning comes from what you do with that insight."

Thomas looked up, puzzled. "What do you mean?"

"Reflection," Leah tossed off casually. "It is the first step to learning becoming embedded into action. Think about it; how often do we take that quiet moment really to consider what we've learned before leaping onto the next thing?

Thomas paused for a moment. "Honestly, very rarely. I'm typically so busy trying to address the problem that I hardly ever take a step back."

"And that's where teams mess up," Leah said. "This is the difference between what is called single-loop learning and double-loop learning," Leah began. "In a single-loop learning mode, an individual rarely questions the broader context. In most cases, they will look to solve problems using established guidelines. For example, the team might look at your Plexon product and simply want to adjust the pricing without examining to see if the product still meets your customer's needs." Leah continued.

Thomas's eyes widened as he held his delicate teacup suspended in the air while in the process of taking a drink. "How did you know that is what the team suggested?" Thomas asked, peering over the top of his cup.

Leah's smile widened with Thomas's question. "For teams unfamiliar with the learning discipline, it is not uncommon to have a single-loop learning mindset." Leah offered in a comforting tone.

"When a team deploys a double-loop mindset, they work to leverage their critical thinking skills to question old assumptions and systems. They dig deep to unpack the why behind the way things are." She continued. "Thinking back helps us connect the dots. It's when we question our thoughts, rethink our game plan, and decide what to do next that is what it looks like to deploy double-loop learning."

"So, it's not just about hearing feedback, it's about figuring out what it really means?" Thomas asked. "Then, the team should be reexamining whether the Plexon still aligns with the market in addition to our larger organization strategy?" Thomas noted, thinking out loud.

"Absolutely," Leah said calmly, reassuring Thomas's thinking.

"The Learning Discipline is anchored through purposeful reflection. If you don't do it, all you're doing is collecting data. But once you actually reflect, you start seeing patterns and themes. That is where the real learning takes place." She added.

Leah paused for a moment, allowing her words to sink in.

"Think of it like this: reflect on what you've experienced, rethink any beliefs that may hold you back or reinforce any that may keep you moving, and then act on those insights. It's a continuous cycle," she explained as she made a circular motion with her finger on the table.

Leah leaned back, teacup in hand. "You know, Thomas, I am still baffled when hearing from a colleague about how teams screw up because they cling to these old ways of thinking. They hang on to those old stories that shape their mindset without them even realizing it. Taking a step back and thinking things through helps us catch those assumptions so we can challenge them and grow."

Thomas nodded, reflecting on the views of his team. "So, reflection is not just about looking in the rearview mirror, but also about finding what holds us back and seeking ways to move forward."

"Yes, Leah added. When you combine reflection and action, you unlock learning in culture, and that's how great teams actually improve. **Everything starts with the ability to learn, unlearn, and relearn.** The question you should be asking is, what old stories, beliefs, or assumptions might we be holding onto that could hold us back?"

The Barriers to the Learning Discipline

Thomas looked around the café, observing people swapping ideas and chatting. "What stops teams from doing this? From staying in Learning Discipline?"

"Fear," Leah said promptly, pouring herself another cup of tea. "Fear of being wrong. Fear of looking weak. Fear of loss. The Noble Prize behavioral economists Kahneman and Tversky noted that loss aversion suggests the pain of losing is psychologically about twice as powerful as the pleasure of gaining," she continued, "It's just easier to stick with what we know, even if it's not working than to admit we might need to grow."

She paused, letting Thomas absorb her words. "That's why leaders have to go first. When you're willing to be vulnerable and admit what you don't know or where you've made mistakes, you show your team that learning isn't just safe. It's necessary."

Thomas's Breakthrough

A few days later, Thomas gathered with his team in the conference room. The atmosphere was somewhat awkward, as his team hadn't really talked things out for weeks, and he could feel their reluctance. "First of all, I just want to say thanks to all of you for sharing your thoughts on leadership and followership," Thomas began. "I know it wasn't easy, and I really appreciate your honesty."

He glanced around the room, his eyes locking with each of theirs. "You know, I kind of realized recently that, even less than leading well, I have not exactly mastered what it's like to be a good follower. Because I get so ahead in leading, I totally spaced on listening and letting you step up when it's the right time."

The room was silent for a second until one of his teammates spoke up. "It's not just you, Thomas. We've been waiting for you to let us know what to do instead of taking the lead ourselves."

Thomas nodded. "Alright, let's switch that up. From now on, I want us to make learning part of everything we do. That means asking questions and sharing ideas. We're in this together."

He looked around the table, making eye contact with each team member. "So, I have a simple question I want us to wrestle with this morning," Thomas began as the team leaned in. "What beliefs or assumptions might we be holding onto that might require us to unlearn or reframe?"

There was a quick pause before one team member chimed in, "It kind of feels like we're all doing our own thing without a clear direction."

Another one nodded. "And we're not really sure who's in charge of what."

Thomas then wrote what they said on the white-board: "Right, this is good. These are the patterns that we have to address. Now, let's think through how we handle these. How can we make those roles and priorities clearer so people are all on the same page?"

The conversation was super lively, with everybody chipping in their ideas and suggestions. By the end of the meeting, Thomas felt more focused and had a plan to move ahead.

For the first time in weeks, Thomas felt like a weight had been lifted off his shoulders. His team wasn't flawless, but they were eager to learn, and that was good enough.

Thomas's Journal Recap

Learning Discipline: Lessons from Leah

Key Insight

Learning is the foundation of optimized teams. It begins with reflection and grows through curiosity and action. Double-loop learning is key to the learn–unlearn–relearn process. Personal mastery, the practice of self-reflection, and a commitment to lifelong learning are essential for individuals to lead themselves and their teams effectively.

Big Takeaway

Learning Discipline begins with curiosity and vulnerability. Learning isn't just about gathering information, it's about connecting the dots, rethinking existing stories and mindsets, and acting on insights.

- Cultivate a Habit of Reflection.
- Adopt Double-Loop Learning.
- Embed Learning into Team Processes.

Steps I'm Taking

- Not assuming everyone knows what I know at the same level I know.
- Refusing to believe I don't know all there is to know about everything we are working on.
- It is essential to distinguish that others on the team may know information but may not fully understand how they make an impact

The Follower Effect

Key Lesson on Followership: As a follower, learning begins with curiosity. It's my responsibility to seek growth, reflect on past experiences, and actively engage in gaining knowledge. By staying open to new perspectives and unlearning old habits, I contribute to the team's ability to adapt and innovate.

Key Lesson on Leadership: As a leader, I set the tone for learning by modeling curiosity and vulnerability. Encouraging questions, creating opportunities for reflection, and valuing diverse viewpoints fosters a culture where continuous learning thrives. Leadership isn't about having all the answers, it's about creating an environment where the team feels safe to explore and grow.

Chapter 3

The Clarity Discipline

Thomas arrived at the park early Saturday morning, the cool autumn air invigorating as the sun peeked through the canopy of golden leaves. Leah sat at a picnic table under a sprawling oak, a thermos of tea beside her and a notebook in front of her. She glanced up as Thomas approached, her serene demeanor radiating calm.

"Morning, Thomas, right on time," she said, gesturing for him to join her. "How's the team doing?" Leah felt a tremendous sense of purpose in this season of life investing in others as The Professor had done with her, all the many years before.

Thomas sighed as he sat down. "Better, I think. The learning exercise definitely helped. We've started asking more questions and reflecting on what's holding us back. But there's still a sense of... disconnection. It's like we're all working hard, but not together."

Leah nodded, pouring herself a cup of tea. "That's because learning is only the first step. Once a team starts to reflect and rethink, the next challenge is turning those insights into alignment. That's where the Clarity Discipline comes in."

What Is Clarity Discipline?

Leah leaned forward as she produced a blueberry scone from the paper bag next to her. She placed it on the napkin and put it in front of Thomas. "Here, this will help as you process this morning." She said with a wink and grin, her tea steaming gently in the crisp air.

"Clarity Discipline is about creating shared understanding. It's when a team aligns on their goals, roles, and expectations so everyone pulls in the same direction," Leah noted. "The Clarity discipline is essential as it adds meaningfulness to the role, which is a critical cognitive mindset for people" she continued.

Thomas frowned. "We've had meetings about goals before, but it doesn't seem to stick. People still end up working on different priorities."

"That's because clarity is more than just about saying the right things once," Leah explained. "It's a constant intentional practice. Great teams revisit clarity regularly because confusion creeps in easily, especially when life gets busy or stressful."

Thomas nodded as he took his first bite of the flakey scone. His eyes lit up with surprise as the hint of lemon both surprised and complimented the flakey texture and fresh, still warm, blueberries that melted in his mouth. Leah couldn't tell if his acknowledgment was for the scone or the conversation but offered a reaffirming smile as she, too, delighted in a bite of the heavenly pastries.

She pulled out her notebook, flipping to a page filled with her distinctive handwriting. "Think of clarity as the team's compass. Without it, everyone sets off in slightly different directions, and you're miles apart before long. This is the *Rule of 2 Degrees.*"

Leah picked up her pen and drew two lines in her notebook, starting from the same point but gradually diverging.

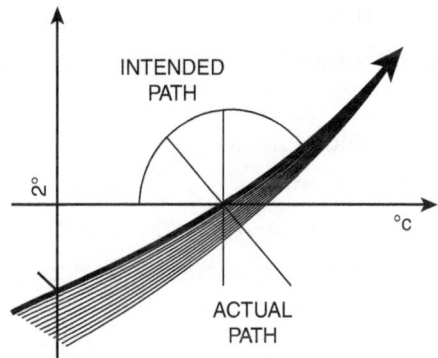

"This," she said, "is the 2-degree rule. At first glance, being off by just 2 degrees doesn't seem like a big deal.

But over time, that tiny misalignment can lead you miles off course. Imagine a plane heading for New York from Dallas but being off by just 2 degrees, it might land in Philly instead. The same is true for teams and individuals. Small slips in clarity or consistency, unquestioned assumption here, a conversation not had there may feel at the time like it will not make much of a difference. Still, they build, pulling you farther and farther off course."

She waited a minute to let the thought sit as her eyes met Thomas'. "This is why clarity and regular recalibration are a must. Clarity becomes your compass, which you absolutely must have in order to hold onto your goals and go along as one with your team toward those goals. Without that, little misunderstandings, or even just a lost emphasis, can easily send the team into frustration, non-productivity, and overlooked opportunities."

"The 2-degree rule reminds you that deliberate alignment is a process, not a check-the-box-and-forget-it activity. It's about reflection, communication, and a shared commitment to course-correct the moment you feel even the slightest drift."

Leah leaned back on the park bench and added, "The best teams know that drift is inevitable. Life moves fast, projects morph, and distractions set in. But when you make clarity a habit, revisiting progress made regarding your goals, roles, and metrics regularly, you give yourself the tools to catch that drift early and stay on course."

Why Teams Struggle with Clarity

Thomas leaned his head in curiosity. "Why is it so hard to get everyone on the same page?"

"Because clarity requires work and exposure," Leah answered. "It is easier to assume that because people 'know' it is good enough. This assumes a learning trap – that everyone gets it. **Never mistake knowing for understanding.** It will only lead to more blame and less accountability" Leah said, looking over her cup of tea. "Sadly, when leaders aren't clear themselves, they tend to avoid pressing for clarity from others." She said this with a tone that suggested this was hard-earned wisdom. Sipping her tea, her eyes expressing deep reflection, "But the cost of ambiguity is high. Teams lose time, energy, and trust when they're confused about what is important and why along with the role they play in accomplishing it."

Thomas nodded slowly. "That sounds like Project Leprechaun. We have five people, and I'm not sure any of us really know who's responsible for what."

"That's a classic clarity issue," Leah said. "When roles and goals aren't clear, teams start to overlap, or worse, disengage."

How to Achieve Clarity

"I'm curious Thomas, what's unclear on your team," Leah prompted.

Thomas's eyes drifted up and to the right as he pondered the question. "I mean, we all know we need to fix Plexon's sales," he began.

"That's the goal, but is it clear," Leah quizzed.

"Well…I'm not sure we have really defined what 'fixing' means," he said with a sheepish grin.

"And, what about roles," she continued.

"I mean, we have them, sort of," Thomas admitted with a hint of hesitation.

"They may know their role." Leah offered expressing a one-handed air-quote. "But, do they fully understand why they are in those roles? Why they matter?"

Thomas let out a low groan as he shook his head in surrender.

"It's okay Thomas," Leah said as she leaned forward, her voice steady and deliberate. "For the majority of teams, clarity starts with answering some basic "what and why" questions:

- What are we trying to achieve?
- Why me (what is my role)?
- Why now?
- Why do it this way?
- Why is it important?
- What is the evidence of progress and success?

Thomas scribbled furiously in his notebook. "Okay, but how do I get my team to buy into this? They're already frustrated, and I don't want to make it worse."

"This is why the Learning Discipline is essential. You involve them in the process through the lens of learning," Leah said simply. "Clarity isn't something you impose; it's something you build together. Start by bringing your team into a discussion. Ask them to help define your goals, answer the essential 'what and why' questions, assign responsibilities, and establish metrics. When people contribute to clarity, they're more likely to commit to it."

Clarity in Action

The following Monday, Thomas brought his people together in the conference room. As he walked to the whiteboard in the room, he wrote six what/why questions on the board.

"I need your help in answering these questions." Thomas began with a hint of humility in his voice. "I recognize that while I think we all know these answers, I am not sure even I am completely clear on all of them." He continued.

Silence.

Someone finally muttered, "Didn't we already discuss this," said the person without looking up as they gently leaned back in their chair as to not be seen by Thomas.

"Not exactly," Thomas said. "The last time we discussed this, we talked about goals, but I let you down by stopping the conversation short."

The last comment raised a few eyebrows as people began to lean forward in their chairs. "I've learned that it is one thing to know an idea but it is something completely different to understand it," Thomas continued.

From the side of the room someone spoke up, saying, "Grow Plexon's sales, right?" "The answer to the first question is grow Plexon's sales." The voice continued with increasing confidence.

"Yes, but let's get specific. What would be evidence of progress, and what does success look like? Is it hitting a certain revenue target? Expanding into new markets? Let's define it."

The team started brainstorming, and their initial hesitation turned into a lively discussion. By the end of the meeting, they had agreed on three clear project outcomes.

Next, Thomas discussed roles. "Who owns each of these pieces of the puzzle?" he asked. "Let's ensure everyone clearly understands their responsibilities so we are all accountable to each other for the outcome."

Each team member volunteered for specific tasks, and Thomas helped ensure the responsibilities were clear and aligned with each person's strengths. This discussion brought renewed energy to the group as they saw how their individual roles contributed to the bigger picture.

Thomas then pointed to the next questions on the board. "Why now? Why do it this way? Why is it important?"

During these questions, the team understood the need to act on Plexon's dropping sales to keep the company relevant in the market. They also discussed why their suggested strategy was appropriate, and how it tied in with the overall strategy of the company. Last but not the least, they also explained the relevance of their work, meaning the importance of the work done by the team not only for the company but also for the personal development of the team members as well as for the collaboration between the team members.

Finally, Thomas looked at the third and the last question – "What is the evidence of progress and success?" he began. "Then how do we know that we are achieving the goals that we have set and the objectives that we have taken?" he asked.

The team listed some of the measurable aspects such as the increase in sales per week, the customers' feedback, and other internal targets that had been met. By the end of the meeting, the team had a good understanding of how they are going to measure their success.

For the first time in weeks, Thomas could feel that there was hope in the room. The team came out of the meeting with a better focus and motivation since they all had a higher sense of purpose for what they were working toward and why.

Leah's Wisdom

A week later, Thomas joined Leah for another campus walk. As they walked around the library, he was reciting his team's progress. "Just by answering the six clarity questions, everything seems to feel better."

"It is," Leah agreed. "Clarity is like a muscle. The more you use it, the stronger it gets. Keep revisiting those questions. And don't be afraid to apply the *2-degree check-in* by asking them again before there is drift."

Thomas nodded, and with his notebook already in hand, he began to jot down notes. "Got it. What's next?"

Leah smiled. "Next week, we'll talk about the Safety Discipline. Because even with clarity, a team can't thrive without feeling a sense of safety."

Thomas's Journal Recap

Clarity Discipline: Lessons from Leah

Key Insight

Clarity starts when you answer the six foundational questions. These questions guide teams to align their goals, roles, and metrics, fostering focus and collaboration.

Big Takeaway

Clarity is not a one-time event; it is a process. Using the 2-degree check-in to give ongoing attention to the six questions ensures team alignment and keeps them adaptive with less drift.

The Six Clarity Questions

- What are we trying to achieve?
- Why me (what is my role)?
- Why now?
- Why do it this way?
- Why is it important?
- What is the evidence of progress and success?

Steps I'm Taking

- Regularly revisit the six clarity questions with my team.
- Ensure every team member knows and understands their role and how it contributes to the larger goal.
- Use the "Why" questions to challenge assumptions and refine strategies.
- Establish measurable evidence of progress and success.
- Create space for ongoing discussions to maintain alignment and joint accountability.

The Follower Effect

Key Lesson on Followership: As a follower, I promote clarity by seeking alignment to the mission and goals of the team. Owning the goals, roles, and progress for me helps the team thrive.

Key Lesson on Leadership: As a leader, I model clarity by facilitating discussions around the six questions. Leadership requires creating a shared understanding, encouraging participation, and ensuring every voice is heard. True leadership is about enabling alignment and empowering the team to thrive.

Chapter 4

The Safety Discipline

Thomas checked his phone to ensure he was at the right location. His message from Leah was to meet at this address, which, as it turns out, is the Arboretum. He hadn't visited this location since a middle school field trip. Walking through the tunnel toward the entrance, he was immediately taken in by the full-wrap mural of floras.

Once inside the Arboretum, he found Leah waiting in her long charcoal gray driving coat with a bright red scarf and thermos in hand.

"Good morning, Thomas. Welcome to one of my favorite spots in the city." Leah began with a beaming smile. "I thought a stroll through the grounds would be beneficial for our chat today," she continued.

Thomas returned the smile as he extended his hand to greet Leah. "I have to admit, flowers were not on my agenda today," he said, with a hint of amusement in his voice.

"You might be surprised how much nature can teach us about teams" Leah said with a wink as she directed Thomas toward the main path leading through the grounds. "Tell me about your week." She asked as the two began a slow stroll along the crush granite pathway.

"The team is making progress in getting clear around what we need to accomplish," he began. "What has stood out this week is how meaningful the work is once we made the connection for each person as to how they impact the work," Thomas said with a sense of satisfaction.

"Yes, significance is important for individuals," Leah replied. "We all need to have a sense that what we do matters," she continued. "Even so. It is equally as important to be able to accomplish your work in a safe manner." She said as she paused in her walk as a way to make a point.

Thomas stopped to gather in the point Leah was making. The look on his face alerted Leah to continue.

"Safety comes in several forms, each important for different reasons," she began. "First, we should never take our physical safety for granted. Some teams depend on physical safety every day" Leah said with a decided tone.

"Then there is the emotional and psychological safety that we need to stay fully engaged in our work," Leah said as she began to walk through the curated colors of plants and flowers.

"I have heard of psychological safety but admittedly, I'm not too sure about what it all means," Thomas said, displaying a bit of vulnerability.

"I appreciate your transparency, Thomas," Leah offered. "For this type of safety to occur, there needs to be some work done on the front end. Beginning with faith and trust," Leah added as she paused once again.

"Trust, Thomas," Leah started, "is like this garden. It doesn't just appear, it must be cultivated. And just like these plants, trust starts with the soil: faith."

Thomas cocked his head to the side, interested in Leah's last word. "Faith?" He asked.

Leah knelt to touch the rich soil. "**Yes, faith. It's the groundwork, the belief that something better is possible even when you can't see it yet.** Without faith, nothing can grow. But even the best soil won't produce anything unless it's nurtured."

Thomas nodded slowly. "So, nurturing the garden is how we grow trust?"

"Exactly," Leah said. **"Trust grows through four seeds: competence, character, consistency, and compassion.** These seeds take root in the soil of faith, but they can only thrive when the environment, the air, water, and sunlight, is healthy. And that's where safety comes in."

Safety: The Air We Breathe

Leah motioned around them. "What do all these plants have in common?"

Thomas looked around. "Sunlight? Water?"

"True," Leah said, "but there's something even more basic: air. Without clean air, none of this would flourish. In a team, safety is like the air we breathe. It surrounds everything. Without it, trust can't grow."

She pointed to a clump of wildflowers that were in bloom, free to grow as they wanted. "Psychological safety is the climate that allows people to be free to be themselves, take risks, share ideas, and yes, even to make mistakes without fear of judgment or retaliation.

It's the linchpin for all other forms of safety. Without it, fear creeps in like a pollutant, stifling growth and silencing voices."

Thomas furrowed his brow. "What about physical and emotional safety? How do those fit in?"

Leah smiled. "Great question, Thomas. Psychological safety is what makes the other forms of safety possible. When people feel safe to speak up without fear of retaliation, they're more likely to call out physical risks or address emotional concerns. It creates the conditions where every voice is valued and every risk – whether physical or emotional – is managed collectively."

She continued, "Think of psychological safety as the air we breathe, physical safety as the water we drink, and emotional safety as the sunlight we absorb. All are essential to grow, but it's psychological safety that binds them together."

"Thomas, safety isn't just a leader's responsibility. It's everyone's. As a follower, you contribute to safety by listening, respecting others, and encouraging vulnerability. When a leader models this, they set the tone for the entire team."

The Four Seeds of Trust

"So, how do we grow our safety?" Thomas asked as he dug into his backpack for his notebook.

Leah smiled, recognizing Thomas exercising his learning discipline. "Planting the right seeds, of course," Leah said with an eager tone in her voice.

Thomas nodded, acknowledging the obvious metaphor.

As they strolled through rows of flowering plants, Leah began. "If you had to put your team's level of trust on a scale of one to ten, with one being no trust, what score would you give the team?" Leah asked with a curious tone.

Thomas squinted slightly to think. "Maybe a 6." He offered in a less than convincing tone.

"If I asked you what you could do to increase that number, would you have an answer?" Leah quizzed.

Thomas scrunched his face while he nodded, indicating he had no idea.

"Don't feel bad, Thomas. Most don't know," Leah offered to comfort Thomas as he jotted down notes as the two continued their stroll.

"Trust is belief in someone or something's reliability to deliver with positive intent based on experience," Leah began. **"Where psychological safety is the feeling that those actions won't result in negative consequences."** Leah continued.

"That said, trust is preceded by faith, which we will discuss further in a moment" she offered with a reassuring grin.

"Trust isn't something you simply declare, Thomas. It's something you cultivate, like a garden. And just like these plants, it starts with seeds – small acts of faith."

She stooped, took a handful of dirt, and watched it slip through her fingers. "Faith is like the soil. It's the substance. Without it, nothing can grow. But even the richest soil needs nurturing."

Thomas nodded, intrigued. "And nurturing trust, what does that look like?"

"It starts with the four seeds," Leah said. "They're like the nutrients every garden needs to thrive: *competence, character, consistency, and compassion.* Let me explain."

Leah led Thomas to a row of climbing roses winding elegantly around a trellis. "The first seed is competence," she said, touching a strong, steady stem. "Your team needs to trust that everyone has the skills to do their part. Without competence, trust topples like a poorly rooted plant."

Next, Leah pointed to the trellis. "This represents character. It's about staying true to your values and commitments. Character gives trust something sturdy to hold onto."

They moved to a patch of daffodils swaying in the breeze. "Then there's consistency," Leah continued. "Just like these flowers bloom year after year because conditions remain steady, trust needs reliability, actions that align with words, day in and day out."

Finally, Leah knelt by a vibrant cluster of wildflowers. "And this is compassion," she said softly. "For many, it's the most important as it represents the care and empathy we show one another. Compassion reminds your team that they are valued as people, not just contributors."

Overcoming Weeds in the Garden

Thomas stopped at a patch of wilting plants. "What happens when trust is broken? Can it be fixed?"

Leah looked curious as she processed Thomas's question, wondering if this question was more about Maya or the team. "This sounds like a question from personal experience," she replied with a hint of curiosity as she continued.

"It can, but it takes care. Start by pruning, acknowledge what's not working. Then, replenish the soil: interpret the moment with those who trust that has been broken, and seek to discover which of the seeds of trust has been damaged the most. You must consider that others may be more in need of a particular seed than you. It requires you to uncover if competency, character, consistency, or compassion has been compromised. Then recommit to restoring those seeds through vulnerability and accountability. Trust can recover, but it requires deliberate effort," she offered, realizing she may have answered a question unrelated to Thomas's team.

Leah crouched beside a cluster of particularly vibrant flowers. "One consideration to not be overlooked is the weeds. Be careful of the weeds." Leah said with a hint of firmness in her tone as she gently pulled on a weed, extracting it from the soil.

"What do you notice," Leah asked, extending the freshly pulled weed.

Thomas closely examines the specimen before pronouncing with a sense of confidence, "It's the roots, they are incredibly deep for such a small weed."

"Exactly. Some look beautiful but can choke out other plants if left unchecked for too long. On a team, this might look like the 'brilliant jerk', someone who delivers results but damages trust. They disrupt psychological safety and erode the culture." She added with an increasing tone to drive home the significance of the point. "The brilliant jerk isn't just a problem – they become a broader story of what has been tolerated."

Thomas frowned as he let out a sigh. "What do you do about them?"

"You confront the weed," Leah said firmly. "Address the behavior directly, and don't let results overshadow relationships. If left unchecked, the weed will suffocate the trust you've worked so hard to grow."

Recognizing and Addressing Weeds

Leah crouched beside the patch of weeds and gently pulled one from the soil. "It's not just about removing the weed, it's about understanding why it grew in the first place. Sometimes, weeds thrive because the soil isn't healthy or the gardener isn't paying attention. On a team, the brilliant jerk might flourish because followership has atrophied or outcomes have been prioritized over relationships, all of which produce ambiguity and equivocality within the culture that tells the wrong story."

Thomas watched her thoughtfully. "So, it's not just their fault, it's about the climate we've created."

"Exactly," Leah said. "**Addressing the brilliant jerk is about two things: having the courage to call out harmful behavior and creating a climate where being a resolute leader and follower is non-negotiable**."

The Role of Faith in Trust

As they continued walking, Leah turned back to the soil. "Remember, Thomas, trust begins with faith. **Faith is the belief in what's possible, even when you can't see it yet. Trust is built when you act on that belief, when you show up, nurture the seeds, and create the conditions for growth**."

Thomas nodded, picturing his team as a garden taking shape in his mind. "Faith is the soil, safety is the air, and trust is what grows," Thomas affirmed.

Leah smiled. "Exactly. And just like a garden, trust requires ongoing care. Tend to it every day, and it will thrive."

Thomas's Journal Recap

Safety Discipline: Lessons from Leah

Key Insight

Safety is the air a team breathes, it surrounds every interaction and makes trust and collaboration possible. Without safety, fear creeps in, silencing voices and stifling growth. But safety doesn't exist on its own, it begins with faith, the belief in potential and unseen possibilities, and grows through trust, cultivated by consistent actions.

Big Takeaway

Faith is the soil on which trust is planted, and safety is the environment in which it thrives. Physical and emotional safety ensure people feel secure and valued, but psychological safety enables teams to take risks, share openly, and grow together.

Steps I'm Taking

- **Start with Faith:** Begin each interaction by believing in the potential of my team, even when results or progress are unclear. Faith lays the groundwork for trust and safety to flourish.

- **Cultivate Trust:** Build trust through consistent actions demonstrating competence, character, consistency, and compassion. Trust grows when I align my words with my actions.

- **Model Safety:** Create an atmosphere of psychological safety by admitting mistakes, inviting feedback, and ensuring every team member feels heard.

- **Reinforce Connection:** Use moments of vulnerability to strengthen the connection between team members, reminding them that their contributions are valued and essential.

The Follower Effect

Key Lesson on Followership: As a follower, I contribute to safety by bringing faith into my interactions, faith in my leader, my teammates, and myself. My actions, like encouraging openness, listening actively, and addressing conflicts constructively, create the trust necessary for the team to thrive.

Key Lesson on Leadership: As a leader, I have to model the connection between faith, trust, and safety. By believing in my team's potential, demonstrating trust through consistent actions, and fostering psychological safety, I create the conditions for growth and collaboration. Leadership is less about control and more about cultivating an environment where people can flourish.

Chapter 5

The Connection Discipline

Thomas shifted his bag on his shoulder as he entered the university library. Admittedly, it had been a while since his last visit to a university library, his last time being a cram session before a final. Leah had chosen this location specifically for their next meeting. The library has a plethora of rooms and additions that have been added since the original building was erected during the mid-century. Each room is adorned with the names of donors who have invested in the school's future. The Centennial Reading room was the perfect retreat from the calmer activity that occupied most all the study areas.

A week had passed since their conversation about trust, and though Thomas's team was starting to open up, he couldn't shake the feeling that something was still missing.

Leah sat in the leather club chair surrounding the marble and iron table tucked in the far corner of the book-lined room. Her notebook was as ever-present as her calm demeanor. She looked up as Thomas approached, smiling warmly.

"Good morning, Thomas," she greeted as she folded the book she was reading closed and placed it on the table. "How's the team?" she asked, motioning for Thomas to join her.

Thomas sat down, exhaling profoundly but in a hush to respect the setting. "Better. The safety-building exercises are starting to make a difference, but I feel like we're not fully connected yet. People are still holding back like they're doing their jobs but not really leaning into the team."

Leah nodded knowingly. "That's because safety is just one discipline that requires the next discipline, *connection*. **Connection is the center hub that holds all the disciplines together**," Leah began. "If you will pardon the pun, but the connection discipline is what connects the other disciplines together," she said with a wry smile. "As humans, we are wired for connection. When it doesn't happen, we become less effective due to increased physical and psychological influences," Leah noted.

Thomas perked up to ask his question, "Connection seems simple to understand, but I am starting to believe there might be more to it than I first thought."

Leah's warm smile communicated all Thomas needed to know. "That is very insightful, Thomas," Leah began.

"Social connection encompasses three parts: your structure or scaffolding, the fulfillment quotation, how well connections fulfill emotional, informational, and practical requirements, and finally, the quality of those connections, either positive or negative," Leah noted as she pulled out her notebook.

What Is Connection Discipline?

Leah opened her notebook and drew three concentric circles. "Connection Discipline is about creating relationships that energize and sustain a team. It's where collaboration becomes seamless, growth becomes intentional, and emotional support becomes real."

Thomas leaned forward. "How do you actually build that kind of connection?"

"Through a community of three types of people," Leah said, pointing to the circles. "*Collaborators, Coaches,* and *Counselors*. Each plays a unique role in fostering connection, and each has a process that makes it work."

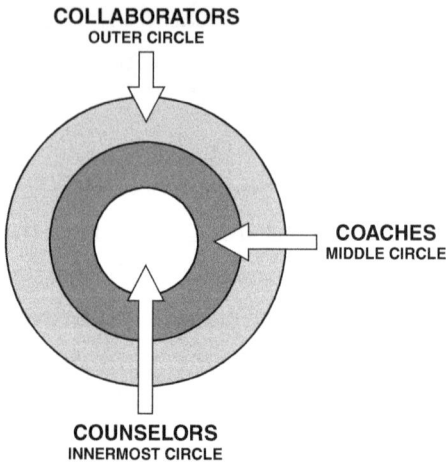

Collaborators: The Team

Leah tapped the outer circle. "Collaborators are people around you but are most often your team, the people you work with daily. Collaboration isn't just about working together. It's about participating in life together."

"Okay," Thomas said, "but what does that look like in practice?"

"That is the right question to ask, Thomas," Leah said. "Let's consider what you have already gleaned in your journey to see how that impacts connection through collaboration." She challenged with a smile.

The Collaborator: Beyond the Leader

Thomas leaned back in his chair, contemplating the professor's question. Thumbing carefully through his journal he found his notes from the first class he experienced with Leah.

A smile brightened his face as he looked toward Leah. "It would seem followership has something to do with this discipline." He offered in a steady but somewhat unsure tone.

Leah nodded gently, "Yes, and…" She coaxed.

Thomas's confidence in Leah's affirmation was noticeable as he continued. "My notes from your class remind me that effective followers are independent critical thinkers and active partners who are focused on the mission." He said, his voice hinting at a new level of confidence.

"Excellent!" Leah exclaimed. "So, if I am hearing you, then effective followership is essential to collaboration?" Leah quizzed.

Thomas nodded with a sense of assurance as the pieces were beginning to form a recognizable picture.

"But what would happen if everyone on the team was an ineffective follower, just waiting to be told what to do, or unwilling to think differently about new ideas?" Leah continued.

Thomas grimaced at the question, obviously creating a flashback to a recent experience with his team.

"That's easy. Nothing happens unless the leader forces something to happen," he said with a hint of reluctance in his voice.

Leah nodded, her eyes expressing a sincere understanding with Thomas.

"For collaboration to create a meaningful connection, it has to involve the dynamic interaction and shared responsibility of the duality of leading and following." Leah began. "It is not about static roles or singular leadership as you have experienced in the past. **Teams build connections through collaboration when individuals demonstrate the intellectual humility to lead and follow appropriately.**" She continued as Thomas began to make notes in his journal. "This duality of roles, when fluid, strengthens relationships, fosters trust, and enables the team to achieve greater outcomes than any individual could accomplish alone. **This is what it looks like to**

move beyond the leader, recognizing that leadership is not confined to one person but is a role that shifts dynamically within a team."

As Thomas scribbled in his journal, he raised his hand, a reflex from being emersed in the campus setting. "So, people on the team should be shifting gears, moving in and out of leader and follower mode regularly?" he asked as he looked up for confirmation.

"Precisely," Leah said as she nodded in agreement. "Thomas, don't miss that the safety discipline we discussed previously supports connection and collaboration," she noted. "There is an effortless motion between roles when people understand they are safe for this type of risk-taking," she continued.

Thomas nodded as his pen hovered over the page. "So, it's not about who holds the title of leader, it's about making space for everyone to contribute?" his voice hinted at a tone of realization.

Leah smiled warmly. "Precisely. **Leadership isn't about holding a title; it's about moving beyond being the leader and enabling the team's success through shared leadership**," Leah said as she relaxed back in her chair.

The Hybrid World: Remote Workers

Leah set her notebook aside and leaned forward. "Thomas, we should discuss teams that are not physically together all the time. This can impact connectedness," she began.

"I have two team members who are mostly remote," Thomas added.

"Hybrid teams are part of the new normal and face unique challenges when it comes to connection," Leah offered. "Collaboration can become fragmented when your team is split between in-person and remote. The rhythms of casual conversations in hallways or impromptu brainstorms around a whiteboard are harder to replicate virtually," she said with an nod. "We offer online classes at the university, which is fantastic, but there is a noticeable difference in the teaching and learning process when the students are all together," Leah said with a bit of a sigh. "It's not that learning cannot or does not happen in virtual environments; it is that it is different and requires a distinctive and intentional approach," she continued.

Thomas nodded. "That's exactly what I'm feeling. The remote folks seem to be drifting."

"That's not uncommon," Leah said. "You must replace those lost in-person moments with structured rituals and tools that create a shared sense of presence. For instance, make time for non-task-related connections. Start meetings with personal updates using the one to ten method of checking in, or set up informal coffee chats over video," she began. "Spending time on the personal side of life is essential for connection," Leah noted. "And don't underestimate the power of context-sharing. Use online instant chat programs, project boards and/or weekly video updates so everybody feels plugged into the bigger picture, regardless of location."

She paused and added, "The most successful hybrid teams create a cadence that creates collaboration everyone can feel, whether sitting in the same room or working halfway across the world." Pausing, Leah continued, "However, be aware of over-indexing on virtual chat as a substitute for in-person. It's useful, but it's not a complete replacement," she cautioned.

Thomas lingered to reflect before jotting a note in his journal.

"Three ideas to keep in mind when collaborating," Leah noted. "**Small acts of kindness make a huge impact.**" She began. "**Empathy and grace go a long way in connecting**. And finally, **find ways to give**

back outside the team. Share your kindness with others," Leah noted with a sense of accomplishment.

Coaches: The Guides

Leah moved to the second circle. "Next are coaches, people who help us grow. These could be internal leaders, external professionals, or even peers."

"What makes a good coach?" Thomas asked.

"A good coach closes gaps or sharpens tools," Leah said. **"Their work is focused, time-bound, and intentional.** They walk you through a challenge, creating awareness and understanding, but they don't do the work for you."

Thomas cocked his head. "So, they're not permanent?"

"Yes and no," Leah said. "Coaching is about evolution. Once the gap is closed, the relationship shifts. The person can still be involved in your daily experiences but maybe not in a coaching mode. Here's the key: **coaching is a two-way street. It works only if the person being coached takes ownership of their growth**."

"So, a coach helps improve my ability to succeed?" Thomas asked.

"Excellent, yes," Leah replied. "Not only your ability but your self-efficacy." She paused, noticing the look of curiosity on Thomas's face, signaling him to ask more.

"**Our self-efficacy is the belief we hold in our ability to be successful**. You may have a skill, but if your self-efficacy is low, you are less likely to leverage and benefit from your skill," she noted.

"So, can anyone be a coach, or do I need to hire external coaches for the team?" Thomas hesitantly asked.

Leah grinned, appreciating Thomas's question. "Great question. The answer is, it depends," she said with a smile. "In most situations, the team can and should act as coaches between each other. This sharpens their skills while improving the team's connection through greater psychological safety."

She paused before she continued. "These are moments that are most effective when the challenges are more operational in nature, with the goals aligning closely with internal processes. This assumes the internal coach processes a level of expertise greater than the person being coached and can invest the time required during their daily routine," Leah noted, leaning back in her chair.

Thomas nodded in agreement, recognizing the moments he had been in coaching mode and never connected the dots. "I had no idea how much coaching I have been doing," he offered with a chuckle.

Leah returned the lighthearted gesture as she laughed along with Thomas. "Yes, that happens more often than you think. Sadly, most people don't get full credit for their coaching efforts," she said with a reflective tone.

"How do you overcome that?" Thomas asked.

"Often, it is as simple as creating awareness and interpretation around the concept of coaching. Once people recognize what coaching really is, they can more fully appreciate their role in it," Leah explained.

"So, when do I bring in someone from the outside?" Thomas asked as he prepared his pen to jot down another insight from Leah.

"Stepping outside our familiar surroundings can bring a level of needed clarity that is sometimes difficult to achieve on our own. External coaches offer fresh eyes and experiences, unclouded by internal dynamics," Leah began her voice steady with experience.

"They're especially effective when addressing the personal or interpersonal challenges that might be hindering operational processes."

Leah leaned forward, her tone steady and encouraging. "At the end of the day, coaching is about transformation, people helping people grow, adapt, and take ownership of their journey, both as followers and as leaders. A good coach empowers followership by building self-awareness, internal accountability, and the confidence to contribute effectively to a team. At the same time, they cultivate leadership by sharpening decisive decision-making, adaptability, and the ability to inspire others. But even the best coaches have their limits," Leah slowly continued, allowing Thomas to catch up in his journal.

"There are times when the challenges aren't about skills or strategies but about deeper, more personal obstacles that hinder both followership and leadership." She paused, her voice softening. "That's when we need counselors. **If coaching is about moving forward, counseling helps us understand and address what's holding us back, unpacking the stuff of the past and present to free us to grow into the leaders and followers we're meant to be**."

Counselors: The Unpackers

Finally, Leah pointed to the innermost circle. "At the deepest level, you have Counselors. These are the people who help us unpack the barriers, our 'stuff', that keep us from connecting," Leah began as she stood from her chair.

Thomas raised an eyebrow. "Our 'stuff'?"

"We've been sitting for a while. Why don't we take a walk and unpack this last idea?" she began as she gathered her bag.

Thomas stood to follow Leah down the grand marble stairway that led to the two-story-tall doors that framed the entrance of the historic library.

Upon exiting the doors, they were met with a brisk, cool fall breeze that had even the most harried co-ed donning a hooded sweatshirt emblazoned with the school's mustang mascot. After a few moments, Leah and Thomas made their way to the boulevard, lined with a canopy of century-old oaks.

As they strolled along the well-traveled sidewalk, Leah inquired, "Tell me about your college experience, Thomas. Did you have many friends?"

The laughter from Thomas was noticeable to those passing by, resulting in a curious glance. "You could say that," he exclaimed. "I am still friends with many of the group from my fraternity," he continued with a smile that confirmed his close connection with his fraternity brothers.

"So, you would say you had a group of people that you could spend time just unloading your day with?" she quizzed.

Nodding his head in agreement, he finally spoke, "I still do, now that I think about it," he offered.

Leah motioned to a bench positioned in the only direct streams of warming sunlight. "Would it surprise you if I told you of the last ten students we have passed, research would suggest six of them struggle with loneliness and isolation?" Leah began settling into the bench with a fond deja vu memory from past moments in a similar setting.

The look on Thomas's face was noticeably one of disbelief. As he settled on the bench, he retrieved his ever-present journal as he finally spoke. "This seems hard to fathom. How is it possible to be surrounded by all these people and feel isolated?" he asked with genuine curiosity.

"That's the right question to be asking. Unfortunately, it is complex to answer," Leah began to explain. "There are several factors that could be involved, such as lack of meaning in life or feeling misunderstood," she continued. "There are a host of psychological barriers that may also exist, including an interesting phenomenon called the *hyperconnectivity paradox*," she said as Thomas looked up to better take in Leah's words.

"Hyper-what?" he asked.

Leah smiled at Thomas's question. "Hyperconnectivity," she replied. **"It seems all of our technology can create an illusion of connection when, in reality, it is creating loneliness due to a lack of face-to-face interactions,"** she added.

Thomas shook his head in disbelief as he jotted down a few notes as his head swirled with thoughts. "What about work?" he blurted out as the thought came to his mind.

"The research would suggest that nearly two-thirds of employees feel a sense of isolation either by some form of exclusion or separation," Leah offered.

As she continued, she pulled out her notebook to point to the final circle she had drawn earlier. "This is part of our *stuff*: doubts, insecurities, emotional baggage. Everyone has it, Thomas," she said as she tapped her notebook. "Because of that, we all need a counselor of some sort to help us stay connected," she insisted. "Counselors could be therapists; I like to refer to them as professional unpackers. I have one that has been a meaningful part of my journey for years," she offered in a moment of vulnerability. "Then, of course, there are our everyday unpackers, such as our trusted advisors or even close friends like your fraternity brothers from college. These are people who have demonstrated repeated moments of trust and psychological safety. Their role is to help us process and reflect so we can connect more authentically."

"Sounds deeply personal," Thomas said.

"It is," Leah replied. "Counselors help us become connected to ourselves. And with a deeper understanding of self, we have a broader capacity to understand others and connect with them."

Counselors: Combating Isolationism

Leah shifted the conversation. "But it's not just about logistics, Thomas. Hybrid work has also amplified isolationism, the feeling of being disconnected emotionally, even when we're in a room full of people or digitally connected."

Thomas tilted his head, intrigued. "You mean, people feel alone even though we're constantly on video conference?"

"Exactly," Leah replied as she smiled, able to relate to the comment about video conferencing. "Isolationism is about emotional distance. When people don't feel truly seen or heard, they disengage. That's where Counselors come in, the people who help unpack the personal and interpersonal barriers that keep us apart. When it gets overwhelming, that is when we need professional unpackers," Leah said with a level of empathy that came from a place of experience. "Or we can leverage mentors or trusted colleagues who make space for others to share what's really on their minds."

Leah let the idea settle before continuing: "For hybrid teams, it's crucial to normalize conversations about well-being. Check-in, not just on tasks but on how people are feeling," Leah offered as Thomas continued to write notes. "I make it a practice to ask my teams to name their high emotion and low emotion of the week, never letting them repeat words," she said with a comforting smile.

Thomas's look promoted Leah to continue. "Most people struggle to name the emotion that is consuming them. So, working on naming our emotions puts us in a place to better deal with those emotions," Leah noted. "Create safe spaces for vulnerability, where team members can admit if they're struggling or feeling isolated. And remember, Thomas, as a leader, it starts with you. Model that openness by sharing your own challenges, and you'll see others follow suit."

Forgiveness

Thomas let Leah's words sink in as he continued to write in his journal. "There is one additional barrier to connection that bears unpacking," Leah continued as she leaned back on the bench, staring at the historic campus chapel.

Thomas stopped writing to look up. His curiosity was noticeable as he sat silently, waiting for Leah's next words.

"One of the biggest barriers to connection personally or professionally is forgiveness," Leah said in a matter-of-fact tone, pausing to let the thought set for a moment before she continued.

Thomas gently placed his pen in his journal as he folded it closed to process Leah's comments fully.

"Forgiveness?" Thomas said in almost a whisper.

Nodding gently, Leah replied. "When we hold grudges against people, we choose not to forgive the other person for whatever real or perceived grievance the other person has committed," she began.

"Somethings are hard to forget," Thomas added, in a tone indicating he was holding on to an old story.

Leah nodded in an understanding way, "Just remember. **Forgiveness is not about forgetting. It's about letting go**."

Thomas cocked his head slightly to get a better view of Leah. "Letting go?" he asked.

"Yes, **forgiveness is letting go of resentment, anger, or the desire for revenge toward someone who has wronged you while fostering understanding and compassion**," Leah acknowledged. *"Gandhi once said that forgiveness was an attribute of the strong, noting that the weak could never forgive,"* she continued.

"It is worth noting that often, the person needing forgiveness the most," Leah started, then paused for effect. "Is ourselves."

Thomas's face went blank as his mind raced with thoughts. Thoughts about him and Maya, and thoughts about his team.

"When we withhold forgiveness from others, we impede our ability to connect. When we withhold forgiveness from ourselves, we erode our self-efficacy, hampering our ability to dream, create, and transform," she continued.

Shifting her weight on the bench, Leah positioned herself to look Thomas in the eye. **"Forgiveness isn't just an act of grace; it's a conscious choice that allows us to connect more deeply with ourselves and others**. By letting go of the weight of resentment and self-blame, we open ourselves up to genuine relationships and the courage to create. In our personal and professional lives, forgiveness is the invisible force that unlocks collaboration, empathy, and trust so teams and individuals can move forward with renewed purpose and togetherness," Leah finished as she gently settled back into the bench, staring across the vast campus, reflecting on moments past when she wasted too many years not forgiving herself.

Building Connections

The aging library building still held a level of sophistication for the occupants. The classic design ensured the building's inhabitants would always feel at home in their surroundings. Thomas was all but jumping out of his skin to put into practice the insights he had recently learned, namely connectedness and forgiveness. He convened his team to the conference room and kicked off by pinpointing one of their barriers to progress, lack of connection.

"Prior to getting to the main agenda item," he told them, "I have a question. Why is this project so important to you?"

There was a moment of silence at the outset, yet as Thomas put forward his take on it, his idea about how their joint efforts could pump new life into Plexon, his team gradually came on board. They took turns revealing their motivations, uncertainties, and even frustrations. For the very first time, the environment was less like a formal discussion and more of an open dialogue. Thomas, reading the room, felt the time was right to introduce new learning to the group, and he did it by defining the scaffolding of the project. He depicted the project's structure on the whiteboard, demonstrating the interconnectedness of its constituents.

"We are each a piece in this jigsaw puzzle," he said, showing tasks and goals mapped out on the glass dry-erase board in the conference room.

"Our collaboration is not a mere juggling of blocks, but really, we are building up a solid foundation that carries meaning," he continued.

Keeping the team going without a hitch, Thomas adopted a new weekly routine: Morning sessions would kick off with a quick one to ten discussion, then discussions regarding priorities, which intended to show the team the power of being united, critical points to be dealt with would be brought to the table on Wednesdays, thus, would enable the team to unify, reaching the goal they are all shooting for; on Fridays, the team would use reflections both to cheer and to learn. In the meantime, Thomas also emphasized his point about developing and nurturing the team's growth. He appointed them as informal mentors and coaches to others to tell them how to handle this particular issue, asking them to focus on the strengths of one another. He also brought in a new practice, which was his version of Leah's inspiration; it was a vulnerability circle. Every team member was asked to cite the highs and lows of the week during the reflections on Fridays; these are emotions that they were allowed to confront and examine.

Thomas's Journal Recap

Connection Discipline: Lessons from Leah

Key Insight

Connection is the central discipline that unites all others, creating the scaffolding for collaboration, growth, and emotional engagement. Authentic connections require intentional effort, vulnerability, and forgiveness, and an understanding of the duality of leadership and followership roles.

Big Takeaway

Connection bridges the gap between individual efforts and collective success, by building trust, fostering open communication, practicing forgiveness, and embracing the duality of leading and following. The Connection Discipline is essential for teams to transform into cohesive units capable of extraordinary results.

Practical Steps I'm Taking

- **Scaffold Connection:** Use structured frameworks like shared goals and roles to align the team's efforts.

- **Model Vulnerability:** Share personal reflections and challenges to encourage openness among team members.

- **Foster Collaboration:** Encourage fluid movement between leadership and followership roles to leverage the strengths of each team member.

- **Practice Forgiveness:** Address and release past grievances to create space for trust and innovation.

The Follower Effect

Key Lesson on Followership: Effective followership is about contributing actively to the team's mission while maintaining emotional and psychological safety. By showing up with intellectual humility and curiosity, I can strengthen connections and inspire others to do the same.

Key Lesson on Leadership: Leadership goes beyond titles, it's about creating a climate of connection where collaboration, trust, and growth thrive. Through vulnerability and internal and external accountability, I can model the behaviors that enable teams to achieve their best.

Chapter 6

The Action Discipline

Thomas sat at the café table, the late afternoon sun casting long shadows across his journal. Leah sat across from him, her tea brimming with hot tea.

"I think I see it now," Thomas said finally, tapping his pen on the table. "Each of these disciplines we've talked about, *Learning, Clarity, Safety, and Connection*, they're not just steps. They're… building blocks of engagement. They're all leading to somewhere."

Leah smiled. "Exactly. Execution."

Thomas leaned back. "Execution, where it all comes together."

"Yes," Leah said. "But don't make the mistake of thinking execution is just the last step. Execution isn't a destination; it's a process. It's the engine that drives everything forward, fueled by everything you've built so far."

She turned her notebook to a blank page and drew a large circle with a smaller circle in the middle, dividing it in half on the top half, above the circle she wrote *Engagement*. On the bottom half, below the circle, she wrote *Execution*. The top half, she divided into three sections, doing the same for the bottom half.

"Execution works in three disciplines: Action, Adaptability, and Celebration. Each discipline serves a purpose. Together, they create a cycle that keeps a team moving, learning, and improving."

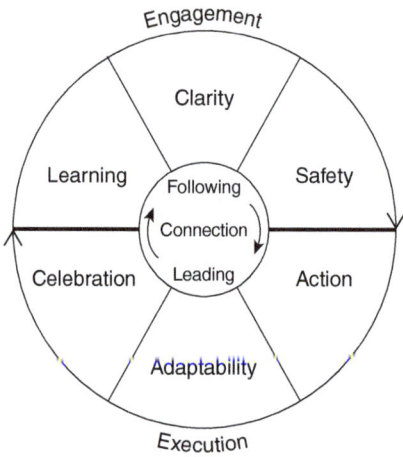

The Foundation of Execution

Leah continued to fill out the circle. "Execution doesn't happen in isolation," she said. "It relies on the foundation you've built:

Learning to keep growing.

Clarity to define purpose and direction.

Safety to create trust and joint accountability.

Connection to sustain collaboration and energy."

Thomas nodded slowly. "So, without those, execution falls apart?"

"Exactly," Leah said. "Teams that try to execute without learning stop adapting. Teams without clarity lose focus. Without trust, they hesitate. And without connection, they burn out. Execution is the culmination of everything we've worked on, and it's what turns preparation into progress."

Decisive Decisions

Leah tapped the first section of the circle. "Execution begins with Action Discipline. This is where plans become motion. But taking action isn't just about working hard; it's about working decisively, aligned, and with momentum."

"Action starts with a decision," Leah said. "And here's the thing: the best teams don't wait for perfect information or total consensus. They make decisions with about 70–80% of the information and commit. Forward motion matters more than perfection."

Thomas jotted down the phrase *70–80% is enough.* "But what if it's the wrong decision?"

"Then you'll adjust in the Adaptability Discipline," Leah replied. "But without a decision, there's nothing to adjust. The Clarity Discipline helps you know what you're trying to achieve, and the Safety Discipline gives your team the confidence to act decisively."

The Polarity Paradox

As Thomas reclined in his chair, the look on his face spoke volumes. Leah leaned in to carefully pour hot water into her teacup and, glancing at Thomas, offering to freshen up his tea. Leah's gesture broke the momentary trance Thomas was in as he processed Leah's last words.

Gently replacing the brass tea kettle on the table, Leah leaned back, crossed her legs, and lifted her teacup to enjoy the smooth, amber-colored tea. The warmth of the drink brought a smile to her face.

Sitting straight in his chair, Thomas came to life as his thoughts began to crystallize.

"You've talked about the need for decisive action, but what about when the decision isn't clear? I feel like some choices aren't just a matter of taking one path over the other, they're more complicated," Thomas began.

"Give me an example," Leah coaxed as she took a nice long sip of tea.

Thomas wasted no time in his response. "Just this week the team had a bit of a heated debate regarding a decision we needed to make."

Leah nodded as she was tracking with Thomas's story. "And the decision?" Leah asked inquisitively.

"The manufacturing plant where Plexon is produced has strict quality controls, but one of our ideas to grow sales would increase production substantially. The team member from manufacturing argued that production capacity is limited based on the quality control systems in place," Thomas continued as Leah began to grin as she saw the direction Thomas was heading.

"Let me guess," Leah began. "You felt the need to choose between quality and production?" she offered.

Thomas sat motionless as he processed Leah's insight. "How did you know?" He asked.

Leah smiled knowingly, still holding her teacup close. "That's because **not every decision is a problem to be solved**, Thomas. **Sometimes a decision is a tension to be managed**," she offered peering over the top of her cup.

Thomas cocked his head to one side. "Tensions? You mean like conflicts?"

"Not exactly," Leah said, leaning forward. "Consider the following: Some circumstances impose clear choices upon us. It's either/or thinking to solve the problem and then go on. For example, what shoes should I wear with this outfit," she said as she motioned to her practical yet stylish shoes.

"Other decisions offer a polarity of sorts whereby the choices seem to be between two competing values, such as producing a quality product while still needing to grow production. In this scenario, this doesn't involve choosing; it requires balancing."

Thomas furrowed his brow. "Balancing?"

Leah picked up her notebook and began drawing. "Let me explain it differently. Your group is trying to decide how Project Leprechaun shall be rolled out: focusing on growing production versus focusing on quality. More product is needed to grow market share, but moving faster to produce more product really gives up some quality. Precision, then, ensures that work gets in the groove, while time is a killer in taking away from production," Leah continued.

"These aren't problems you solve by picking one side," she explained. "They're polarities, both are necessary. You need speed to make progress and precision to ensure quality. The goal isn't to choose, it's to manage the tension between them," she noted very matter-of-factly.

Thomas nodded slowly, his pen moving across the page. "So how do you do that?"

Both/And Thinking

Leah smiled. "Start by recognizing when you're dealing with a polarity. If both sides have clear upsides and downsides and depend on each other for balance, you're in both/and territory." Taking her pen, she drew a square in her notebook and divided it into four equal parts. "Here's what you do next."

"The top half of the chart represents what you want to gain; think of it as the benefits of each side. Production drives sales, while precision ensures quality." Leah began as she continued to illustrate her thoughts in her notebook.

"Then, consider the risks of overemphasizing or over-indexing one over the other, rushing could lead to errors, while perfectionism could cause delays," she continued as she filled in the lower portion of the chart.

"One side of your chart should show the benefits, what we want, from an increase in production at the top, and what would happen should we overemphasize speed, what we don't want. That should be shown at the bottom of the chart," Leah noted as she drew a circle around one side of the chart.

"The other side of the chart shows the positives and negatives of quality." Drawing a similar circle around that side.

"You will notice that the positive of speed is kept in check by the corresponding negative of quality." As she drew a curving arrow from one side to the other. "The same is true for quality; it is held in balance by the corresponding negative side of speed," Leah said as she completed the infinity looping arrows on her sketch.

Thomas's eyes were fixed on Leah's drawing as she effortlessly stretched out her thoughts for Thomas. Pulling out his phone, he snapped a picture of her diagram.

Engaging the Team

Leah beamed as Thomas soaked up the new learning. "For this to be fully successful, you will need to bring the tension out into the open," Leah began settling back in her chair for a brief respite.

Thomas's curious look was followed by an equally exquisite question. "This sounds easy, but how do you bring it out in the open?"

"It begins with awareness," Leah began. "The learning discipline should strengthen the team's curiosity muscle," Leah continued. "Once you have taught them the concept of problems and polarities, you can ask curious questions," she continued.

"So, I could ask, *We need both production and quality, these appear to be polarities, how can we balance them?*" Thomas stated with an increased level of confidence.

"Excellent!" Leah exclaimed. "Invite your team to consider ideas that honor both priorities," she added with a reassuring tone.

Avoiding the Priority Trap

"Remember, managing polarities isn't one-and-done," Leah continued. "You'll have to readjust as the project evolves," she noted as Thomas acknowledged her insights, jotting a note in his journal. "This is where you can fall into the *priority trap* if you're not careful," Leah continued with a tone of caution in her voice.

Thomas's eyebrows peaked as he listened to Leah's warning. "How can priorities become a trap? I thought priorities help keep you out of trouble?" he asked.

"Yes, priorities are an important part of life. Sadly, like problems, people frequently misunderstand or misapply priorities," she noted, tapping her pen on the notebook page.

Understanding the Trap

"The priority trap is sprung with leaders who over fixate on one priority, leading to real or perceived neglect of other elements of the organization that are equally important," Leah began. "This over-indexing is often referred to as *priority fixation* and can lead to a type of tunnel vision for leaders," she noted.

Thomas nodded as he drew quick insights from conversations at his work. He had just listened to the recent leadership town hall, where they discussed the need for cost-cutting in the organization and how this was a top priority. His team immediately began texting him about how that would impact their work on Project Leprechaun.

"We have certainly fallen into that trap in the past," Thomas said with a hint of defeat in his voice. "The last time we had a 'top priority'," he began, using air quotes. "We became fixated on cost reduction, to the point that we took our eye off of customer service by not filling open roles," he continued nodding his head as he made the connection while speaking. "The dynamic nature of priorities would demand a frequent review and recalibration to prevent priorities from becoming static," Leah offered.

Leah leaned forward, her tone steady yet encouraging. "Thomas, managing priorities isn't about setting them once and assuming they'll hold. Priorities must evolve, adapt, and realign as the situation shifts. A priority that never shifts is a value and should be seen as such, thus shifting it to a polarity," she noted matter-of-factly.

"The key is recognizing when a priority serves a purpose and when it becomes a trap, leading the team to neglect other critical dynamics, like managing polarities," she continued.

Thomas nodded, scribbling a note in his journal. "So, it's less about being rigid and more about staying aware and responsive?"

"Exactly," Leah replied with a smile. "Priorities are important, but they're just one piece of the puzzle. True leadership and followership lie in the ability to keep a balanced perspective. It's about knowing when to focus intensely and when to step back to see the bigger picture. This is how you avoid the trap and empower your team to thrive," Leah said with a crescendo of confidence in her voice.

She paused, letting her words settle before adding, "Remember, a team that doesn't understand how to navigate its problems, polarities, and priorities often gets stuck. But a team that learns to integrate these decisive decision tools with an awareness builds resilience. They're able to move forward with clarity, agility, and purpose," she said.

As Thomas closed his journal, he felt a renewed sense of direction. The idea of balancing priorities with polarities and aligning the team's focus wasn't just a concept, it was a strategy he could begin applying immediately. "Thank you, Leah. This changes everything."

Leah smiled warmly. "It's not about changing everything, Thomas, it's about changing how you see what's already there."

Applying It

Thomas tapped his pen thoughtfully. "That makes sense. I think my team has been stuck in this exact tension. Part of us wants to run fast to show progress on something, and another part is holding back to double-check on everything." He said with a hint of exhaustion in his voice.

"And they're both valuable," Leah said. "Here's how you can bring the team together: Acknowledge the tension. Say, *'I see that we're trying to balance production and quality. Let's talk about how to move forward while respecting both'*. You might decide to prioritize production speed for now, but set checkpoints to ensure quality along the way," she noted. "Using the map as a visual can be beneficial for those on your team that are more visual learners," Leah said as she drew a large circle around the map she had created for Thomas.

The Power of Both/And

Thomas smiled as he scribbled down Leah's words. "This is a game-changer. I've been treating every decision like a problem to solve, but some of them are about finding harmony instead," Thomas said with a sense of discovery.

Leah picked up her teacup, smiling. "Exactly. In knowing polarities, you turn a key to the next level of decision-making that respects complexity and leads to more robust outcomes. It's not about taking one path. It's about walking both, with intention." She explained.

Aligned Execution

"Once the decision is made, alignment is everything," Leah said. "Execution falls apart when people don't know their roles or how their work connects to the bigger picture."

Thomas nodded. "So it's about making sure everyone's moving in sync?"

"Exactly," Leah said. "Connection Discipline laid the groundwork for collaboration. Clarity Discipline builds on it by making sure everyone knows their responsibilities, timelines, and dependencies. Think of your team as an orchestra, every instrument has its part, but it only works if everyone plays together."

Sustained Momentum

"And finally, momentum," Leah said. "Action may feel like a sprint, but it's a marathon. You must keep the energy alive through habits like progress check-ins, celebrating small wins and smart failures, and reminding the team why their work matters."

"Momentum seems so fickle," Thomas began. "Just this weekend, I was watching a college football game, and it was apparent when momentum shifted," he noted.

"You are so correct, Thomas," Leah began leaning forward in her chair. "Your sports example is notable," she said, continuing her thought. "Teams can lose momentum if the story suddenly shifts. The sudden change in forward progress tends to jolt the system, causing a person or a team to lose their momentum," she said as someone who recently witnessed a momentum swing.

"So, how do I avoid the swings?" Thomas asked.

"One way is by creating a rhythm for your team that introduces intentional forward progress," Leah said. "Weekly syncs, visible progress tracking, and recognition for what's going well in addition to coaching around what could be better. Momentum is sustained when it is not left to its own inertia, it's something you build intentionally," she stated in a very matter-of-fact tone. "In fact, there are times in sports when a coach will call a timeout should the momentum shift away from the team. This allows the team the opportunity to regroup." Leah continued. "Bottom line, either you manage the momentum, or it will manage you."

Thomas's Journal Recap

Action Discipline: Lessons from Leah

Key Insight

Execution begins with decisive decisions. Teams that wait for perfect information often stall, while those that embrace clarity and momentum create progress. The best decisions come with 70–80% of the information – forward motion is more valuable than perfection.

Big Takeaway

Effective action balances decisiveness with adaptability. Without action, there is nothing to adjust. Action Discipline provides the initial push that moves teams from intention to impact.

Steps I'm Taking

- **Make Decisive Decisions:** Commit to action with the best available information and encourage team alignment.

- **Decision Framing:** Recognize whether challenges are problems to solve or tensions to manage.

- **Sustain Momentum:** Establish check-ins and accountability rhythms to keep initiatives moving.

The Follower Effect

Key Lesson on Followership: Followers contribute to execution by aligning their actions with team goals, initiating progress, and maintaining momentum. Execution is not passive – it requires proactive engagement from every team member.

Key Lesson on Leadership: Leaders empower decisive action by creating clarity and safety. They help their teams move forward confidently, ensuring alignment and focus while making room for adjustments when necessary.

The Action Discipline

Chapter 7

The Adaptability Discipline

R efreshing her tea, Leah retrieved her pen and moved to the second section of the circle. "Action Discipline gets the ball rolling. But execution rarely goes exactly as planned. That's where the Adaptability Discipline comes in," she said as she wrote the word boldly in her notebook.

Situational Awareness

"Adaptability feeds off of your Learning Discipline," Leah explained. "Being constantly curious about what's working? What's not? And why? Feeds adaptability," she stated with a firm tone. "Regular *progress made, and progress needed feedback loops* help you notice when something needs to change before it becomes a crisis."

Feedback Loops

Thomas grinned as he sipped the remaining drops of tea. "We seem to enjoy feedback, to a degree," he beamed.

"Excellent," Leah replied. "Just know, awareness alone isn't enough," she said. "You need a system for acting on feedback, whether that's testing a new approach, shifting priorities, harmonizing polarities, or recalibrating timelines. Adaptability is about learning in real-time and making adjustments without losing momentum."

Strategic Flexibility

"Finally, adaptability requires flexibility," Leah said. "But not just flexibility for its own sake. It's about adjusting the path without losing sight of the destination."

Thomas frowned. "How do you avoid losing focus while you adapt?"

"By staying connected to your team's clarity and safety," Leah said. "Adaptability isn't about abandoning the goal. It's about finding smarter ways to reach it. This is where you leverage your ability to *learn–unlearn–relearn*," she noted as she wrote those words in her notebook, drawing a line under each word for emphasis.

Looking up from her notebook, Leah sat straight up in her chair to make a point. "I once heard the story of a laptop manufacturer that set out to build the thinnest laptop on the market," she began in full story-telling mode.

"The engineering team proudly delivered an ultra-thin prototype to the team leader, who was impressed with the work of the team, but had to point out that the laptop they built was just barely thinner than the competition," she continued, pausing for a dramatic effect.

"When the team leader asked why it wasn't any thinner he was met with a barrage of reasons as to why the laptop could only be this thin."

Thomas's eyes began to widen as he was mentally drawing parallels to his own situation.

"What did the team leader do next?" Thomas asked with a noticeable lean as he was eager for the rest of the story.

"The team leader asked a simple question," Leah began. "What thinking are we holding onto that we need to unlearn?" she said with a tone that hinted to a level of familiarity with this story at a personal level.

"What did they discover?" Thomas asked.

"All they had learned about designing laptops was based on a couple of industry standards that were acceptable by every engineer and designer, mainly the thickness of a key on the keyboard," she continued with a sly grin. "It wasn't until they were willing to unlearn what they knew to be true about the

117

The Adaptability Discipline

design of the keys on the keyboard, and relearn a way to redesign what had been an industry standard, that they were able to reduce the thickness of their thinnest design, by half," she said with a decided emphasis on the last word.

Thomas's eyes remained wide as he looked at his laptop on the table, realizing he was staring at the by-product of Leah's story.

Thomas's Journal Recap

Adaptability Discipline: Lessons from Leah

Key Insight

Adaptability is the counterbalance to action. While action propels a team forward, adaptability ensures they stay on course, adjusting to new insights and obstacles along the way. Without adaptability, action turns into rigidity.

Big Takeaway

Change is inevitable, and teams that embrace feedback loops and strategic flexibility can pivot without losing momentum. Adaptability is not about reacting – it's about proactively refining approaches through checking in on progress made and progress needed.

Steps I'm Taking

- **Build Feedback Loops:** Establish mechanisms for real-time adjustments based on team input and performance.

- **Pivot Strategically:** Shift priorities or timelines as needed while maintaining alignment with overarching goals.

- **Leverage Proactive Adaptability:** Use reflection and curiosity to anticipate adjustments before they become urgent. Ask the question, what might we be holding onto too tightly that might be holding us back?

The Follower Effect

Key Lesson on Followership: Effective followers are observant, responsive, and open to change. Their willingness to adapt strengthens team resilience and creativity.

Key Lesson on Leadership: Leaders cultivate adaptability by fostering a culture where feedback is valued, adjustments are embraced, and learning is continuous. Leaders who manage change with strategic flexibility create teams that are innovative and future-ready.

Chapter 8

The Celebration Discipline

Leah tapped the final section of the circle. "And then there's Celebration Discipline. This is where most teams fall short. They focus on doing the work, but they forget to recognize the progress, reflect on the lessons, and renew their energy."

Acknowledgment

"People need to feel seen," Leah said. "Whether it's a shoutout in a meeting, a team lunch, or a simple thank-you, acknowledgment builds morale and keeps people motivated."

Reflection

"But celebration isn't just about pats on the back," Leah continued. "It's about reflecting on what worked, what didn't, and what you learned. Without that, your team will keep making the same mistakes."

"It should be noted that only reflecting on wins minimizes celebration," Leah began. "It is equally important to reflect and acknowledge the skinned knee moments along the way."

Thomas nodded slowly, recognizing a few skinned knees in his role as team lead. "Doesn't this open people up to admitting failure?" he asked.

Leah's smile provided instant comfort for Thomas as she replied. "When failure is misinterpreted, it is viewed as a negative. When viewed correctly, it is seen as part of the iterative process of learning and growth."

Renewal

"Finally, celebration is about renewal," Leah said. "It's not just looking back, it's preparing for what's next. Taking time to recharge ensures your team is ready for the next execution cycle."

Execution in Action

Back at the office, Thomas introduced the Execution Cycle to his team. He started with Action Discipline, clarifying decisions and aligning responsibilities. As challenges arose, he encouraged feedback loops and small adjustments to keep the team on track. And when the team hit a major milestone, he surprised them with a reflection session, asking, "What did we learn? What can we do even better next time?"

The difference was immediate. The team moved faster, adapted more easily, and found energy in their wins. For the first time, Thomas felt like they were truly executing, not just working.

Thomas's Journal Recap

Celebration Discipline: Lessons from Leah

Key Insight

Execution is not just about action and adaptability – it's also about sustaining energy. The Celebration Discipline ensures that teams don't just work but also acknowledge progress, reflect on learning, and renew their energy for the next cycle. Without celebration, execution becomes exhausting rather than empowering.

Big Takeaway

Momentum isn't just built through action; it's sustained through meaningful recognition, reflection, and renewal. Celebrating wins – both big and small – keeps teams engaged and reinforces the behaviors that drive long-term success.

Steps I'm Taking

- **Acknowledge Contributions:** Express gratitude regularly and recognize both effort and outcomes.

- **Reflect on Progress:** Create intentional space to evaluate what worked, what didn't, and what can be improved.

- **Recharge for What's Next:** Ensure the team has moments of rest and renewal to maintain long-term effectiveness.

The Follower Effect

Key Lesson on Followership: Great followers don't just execute – they celebrate the journey. They encourage team morale by recognizing wins, learning from failures, and reinforcing a culture of appreciation.

Key Lesson on Leadership: Leaders set the tone for celebration by creating moments of recognition, fostering reflection, and ensuring the team remains energized for future challenges. Celebration isn't just about looking back – it's about preparing for what's next.

Chapter 9

The Final Word

Thomas was consumed with his thoughts as he sat in the café, the buzz of afternoon chatter fading into the background. After weeks of spending time with Leah, he couldn't help but smile as he looked at the porcelain teacup in his hand, a considerable departure from his high-fashion coffee drink.

His journal lay open before him, its pages filled with diagrams and notes from the past few weeks. Each page marked a step on his journey: Learning, Clarity, Safety, Connection, Action, Adaptability, Celebration. Together, they had transformed his team and his leadership and followership approach.

And yet, staring at this blank page before him, he couldn't help but feel that something was missing.

"You've come a long way, Thomas," Leah said as she broke the silence, sitting across from him with her ever-present cup of tea. "But where are you taking all this insight?"

Thomas frowned. "What do you mean?"

Leah leaned forward. "You've cracked the code professionally. Your team is thriving. Your organization is on the cusp of something great. But what about personally? What about Maya?"

Her name was like a wave washing over him. He thought about the late-night talks that grew shorter, inside jokes that now felt like a lifetime ago. Somewhere in between, he and Maya's connection had fizzled, and he'd told himself that's just the way things are.

"I don't know if I can fix that," he admitted. "It's complicated."

Leah's Insights on Trust and Faith

Leah smiled softly. "It always is, Thomas. Relationships are messy, but the principles don't change. Learning, Clarity, Safety, Connection – those aren't just for teams. They're for relationships, too. The real question is, are you willing to try?"

Thomas hesitated, staring down at his journal. "I want to, but what if I've already lost her trust?"

Leah's tone was calm but insistent. "Trust isn't just about what's already there – it's about what you're willing to build. And building trust starts with faith."

"Faith?" Thomas exclaimed

"Remember, faith is belief in what you can't see yet," Leah said. "It's the belief that the better possibility might be, even though it's not a certainty. Trust, then, results from the action you take on a belief. Think of this: Faith is foundational, and the trust is the house you build upon it."

The Doubt Inside

Thomas's look told an all too familiar story, one of doubt that was creeping into his thoughts. He gently sat his teacup on the table as he stared, somewhat blankly into the distance as he processed Leah's words.

Smiling, Leah poured tea from the brass pot, the steam curling upward like the strands of a story yet to be told. With a honed precision, she filled both cups, allowing the conversation to breathe before her next words.

"You know, Thomas," she began softly, "people give doubt such a bad name, but it's not the enemy of faith – it's a doorway."

She handed him the cup and let the silence settle momentarily. She watched as he wrapped his hands around the warmth, his eyes fixed on the steam rising into the air.

"There's a story I was told many years ago, one about a man who shares your name, Thomas." Leah began. "Interestingly, he was somewhat like yourself. His doubts almost got the best of him, not because he did not care but because he did, and so he had to be sure." She continued.

Thomas raised an eyebrow, half-smiling. "Doubting Thomas?"

Leah nodded with a wide grin of assurance. "Yes. He needed proof, something tangible to hold onto. The beautiful part is that he was not shamed for that; on the contrary, he was invited in: see, touch, believe. But be sure, faith isn't about having all the answers; no, it's about moving forward despite the questions. That's where trust comes in." Leah explained as she sipped her tea.

Thomas leaned back, her words slicing through the haze of self-doubt he had been carrying. His mind raced as Leah's words settled over him like a warm blanket. *"Could it really be true? Doubt wasn't a*

failure, and my faith can grow, even here?" He won-
dered in his thoughts.

"So, you are saying doubt is not failure?" He asked,
looking for some reassurance to extinguish the anx-
ious sensation he was beginning to feel inside.

"Not at all," Leah said firmly. "It's human. Even the
strongest among us falter when the waves rise, like
Thomas's friend, Peter, stepping out of the boat, to
quote another story from long ago. But here's the
lesson: Faith grows in the reaching. It grows in the
moments we choose to take another step, even when
we're sinking." Leah said with an increasing tone of
assurance in her voice.

Leah waited, letting the weight of her words sink in.

"Maya's faith is bold, containing a persistence that
refuses to quit." Leah continued. "And you, Thomas,
you have a faith that's learning to trust. Both kinds of
faith are powerful, but it's trust that builds the bridge
between where you are and where you're meant to
be," she said confidently as if speaking from a pro-
found personal experience.

For the first time, Thomas let himself consider that
maybe his doubts didn't disqualify him but could, in

fact, be what propelled him. His faith didn't have to look like Maya's or Leah's; it simply needed to take one step forward.

"So, what's the next step?" he asked, his voice lower now, surer.

Leah's eyes softened. "The next step, Thomas, is to keep showing up. Faith doesn't demand perfection, just persistence." Her voice softened in tone as she paused.

Leah let her words linger as her thoughts drifted for a moment. "For me. I find time to intentionally reflect on my personal faith as a Christian. It's in those quiet moments, when I am deliberately pausing to let go of the noise, that is when I sense my spirit being refreshed, like stepping into a cool stream after a long journey. This is where I spend time leaning into my faith," she offered in a tender, caring tone.

"Thomas, trust is built one small act at a time. Start there." She offered. "For you, this might mean sitting with the doubt but taking the next small step. You might need to lean into the discomfort instead of running from it," she said confidently.

The Disciplines Revisited: Trust and Faith in Focus

As Leah spoke, Thomas felt the pieces fall into place. The disciplines he had worked to master professionally weren't just about managing teams – they were about building meaningful relationships. And if he wanted to reconnect with Maya, he needed to apply what he'd learned.

Learning Discipline: Start by Listening

"Start by listening," Leah said. "Not just to her words but to what she's feeling. Reflect on what's changed and what you might have missed. Learning Discipline isn't just about acquiring knowledge – it's about understanding her perspective and being willing to grow from it."

Thomas jotted down the phrase: Listen to understand, not to respond.

Clarity Discipline: Align Expectations

"What are your expectations from this relationship, Thomas? What does Maya expect?" Leah asked. "Clarity isn't just goals – it's how you connect those visions. Are you going toward the same future? What's the evidence it is working, and where may some gaps be?"

Thomas wrote down, *Ask – never assume. Clarity is co-creation.*

Safety Discipline: Building with Faith, Vulnerability, and Trust

Leah's expression softened. "Maya wants to know she is safe with you, not just physically, but emotionally and psychologically." "Establishing that safety starts with vulnerability," she said. "If you want to rebuild trust, you start by creating an environment it can grow in. And that begins with honesty – honesty about your fears, your failures, and what you're willing to do differently."

Thomas nodded but still looked uncertain.

"That's where faith comes in," Leah said. "Faith is the belief that you can rebuild the trust even if you do not know how yet. Trust is what you build once you act upon that belief by showing up repeatedly over time. It's not a point in time, it's a process," Leah added.

Remember the four seeds of trust: competence, character, consistency, and compassion? "Without competence, there is no confidence in each other's abilities. Without character, trust is fragile. Without consistency, it's unreliable. And without compassion, it's unsustainable," Leah said.

Thomas wrote, *Faith gives trust its foundation. Vulnerability builds the framework. But psychological safety is the bond that holds it all together, making trust resilient enough to withstand the strongest storms.*

Connection Discipline: Create Shared Moments

"Connection is about shared moments," Leah continued. "It's not about grand gestures – it's about committing to show up, emotionally and intentionally, even in the small things. Create a rhythm of connection. Just like on a team, consistency and presence matter," Leah noted with a tempering in her tone.

Thomas leaned forward, rubbing his temples, his elbows firmly planted in his knees as he stabled himself from tipping forward. The question had been gnawing at him for weeks. Was he fooling himself? Could he truly balance the demands of leading a team and maintaining a meaningful, long-distance relationship?

His mind replayed past mistakes – missed dinners, half-hearted "we'll talk about it later" responses to

Maya, the unread texts during back-to-back meetings. He had always told himself he was doing it for the future, but what if there was no future if he didn't show up now?

Leaning back, Thomas finally exhaled the long breath he had been holding. "It seems I need to make a choice," he began.

"And what would that be," Leah asked.

"I need to either lean in with Maya or decide to part ways to focus on my career," Thomas said with a strong sense of reluctance in his voice.

Action Discipline: Making Decisive Decisions

Leah studied Thomas carefully. "So, what's stopping you from choosing both?"

Thomas scoffed. "That's just it. If I focus more on my relationship, won't my team suffer? If I double down on my leadership, won't Maya feel like she's always coming second?"

Leah raised an eyebrow. "And who told you those were the only options?"

Leah's gaze spoke volumes; it was time to take action. Thomas shifted side-to-side in his chair as his nervous energy looked for an escape. His mind raced as he processed all that he had learned from Leah, systematically ordering his thoughts as he prepared for the best next step.

Leah tapped her fingers on the table to capture Thomas's attention. "Ever been in a kayak?"

Thomas frowned. "A few times, yeah."

"If you only paddle on one side, what happens?" Leah continued with a quickening pace.

"You go in circles," Thomas replied, noticing Leah's change in tempo and now working to re-engage.

Leah nodded. "Exactly. You need to paddle on both sides – not equally at all times, but in rhythm, as required – to move forward. You're trying to solve this like it's a math problem with one right answer when it's actually about balance and boundaries."

"So, what is it you are trying to solve?" Leah asked with a coaxing tone in her voice.

Thomas settled his energy and sat upright to fully process Leah's question.

"Are you dealing with a problem or a polarity?" she continued.

Thomas smiled as he nodded his head, letting out a bit of a chuckle as a sense of relief washed over his body.

"That's it!" he exclaimed. "I've been trying to solve a problem when the reality is I have a polarity," he continued with an increasing momentum in voice.

"And what is the both/and answer?" Leah prompted.

Thomas took a long deep breath, gathering his thoughts. As he slowly exhaled he calmly said, "That I can be in a meaningful relationship AND manage a successful team. It is not an either/or problem to solve but a tension that needs to be appropriating managed."

Adaptability Discipline: The Ability to Check and Adjust

"But what if I get it wrong?" Thomas said, voice quieter now.

Leah smiled. "You will. The question is, will you adjust when you do?"

Thomas exhaled slowly. He had been so focused on making the perfect choice that he had never considered that navigating both was an ongoing process, not a one-time decision.

Leah's gentle eyes glistened at Thomas's revelation. "This will require a new level of adaptability on your part," she said tenderly.

Thomas was beginning to connect the dots. Leadership isn't about solving problems perfectly but about thoughtfully managing the constantly present tensions with intention. Followership is the flipside of the leadership equation; just as vital, it requires intellectual humility to seek out all sides and the middle while leveraging their influence to create movement. This was true for the relationships on his team, and now it is becoming increasingly clear that the same applies to his relationship with Maya.

Pulling out his phone, Thomas's thumb hovered over the photo icon of Maya. His internal instincts told him to send her a text message, but it was his heart that slowed his hand from tapping the screen.

"What is running through your mind?" Leah asked as she watched Thomas process.

"Everything inside me says send Maya a text," he began with a hesitation.

"And your heart?" Leah prompted.

The Letter

Later that night, Thomas sat down to his desk, his lone lamp casting a soft amber glow over the waiting blank page in front of him. He picked up his pen, hesitated a moment, then wrote:

Dear Maya,

I've been thinking about us lately, about where we are and where we're going, and where I've fallen short. I realize now, on building something for the future, that I haven't been fully present in the moments that matter most, moments with you.

I miss you, Maya. I miss your laugh, your insights, the way you always know the right thing to say when I don't. You challenge me to be the best version of myself, even when I get lost in my own head, you bring clarity. And I know I haven't done enough to show you how much you mean to me.

If I've learned anything recently, it's that relationships – whether at work or in life – don't thrive on autopilot. They take effort, intentionality, and vulnerability to have real conversations. I see now that I haven't created the safe space for those conversations, and for that, I'm sorry.

I don't want to take us for granted. I want to do the work, be more intentional, to ensure we are building something meaningful together. But I also know I can't do that alone. I want to know how you're feeling, what you need, and what you need for the two of us to move forward.

You matter to me, Maya, and I recognize now that the story I have been writing has been a poor example of how I truly feel. When you are ready, I'd love to talk, listen, and discern how to write a story of forever after with you.

With all my heart,
Thomas

The Celebration Discipline: Telling the Story

This moment, this feeling … he had never valued his team at this level before. Leaning back in his chair, Thomas watched his team tell stories and laugh over the scattered plates of comfort food from Bubba's Diner. The room was buzzing with energy, such a contrast to the tension that had been felt among the team only a few weeks ago.

Without such a break, teams operate on fumes. Without time to celebrate and reflect, they miss the lessons in the wins and the skinned knee struggles; without rest, they lack the vigor to take on the next challenge. Leah's words came back to him: "Execution is not just about action and adaptability. It's about sustaining energy. And it's all about relationships."

Thomas stood as the plates were cleared, raised his glass, and said: "I just want to take a moment to thank you; everyone has been a pillar in ways that go beyond the purely material: you have challenged each other, you have made yourselves available, and above all, you have been able to count on one another."

"The work matters, but it is how we do it together that makes the difference," he said as he paused, making eye contact with his team. "I appreciate each of you."

Toward evening, Thomas was back in his favorite café, his notebook open on a fresh page. He reflected on how much the team had changed, not only in its execution but also in its approach to working as a fully connected and engaged team. Before his eyes, Thomas witnessed the team learning and growing into an extraordinary team.

There was still one more person with whom he would like to celebrate. And he took a deep breath, closed his journal, and reached for the telephone. Tapping the number at the top of his favorites list, he lifted the phone to his ear.

Within moments, the voice on the other side brought an instant smile to his face.

"Thomas, what a treat. What's going on?"

"Hey, Maya. Today was fantastic. I couldn't wait to tell you the story."

Appendix
Resource Material

The Prologue

Bridwell, T. (2020). *Saturday morning tea: The power of story to change everything.* B2B Books.

The Words

Bridwell, T. (2022). *The do over: A story about writing your new story.* B2B Books.

The Lecture

Bridwell, T. (2024). *The follower effect: A story about flipping the script on leadership.* B2B Books.

Campbell, J. (1949). *The hero with a thousand faces.* Princeton University Press.

Vogler, C. (2007). *The writer's journey: Mythic structure for storytellers and screenwriters* (3rd ed.). Michael Wiese Productions.

The Learning Discipline

Argyris, C., & Schön, D. A. (1974). *Theory in practice: Increasing professional effectiveness.* Jossey-Bass.

Edmondson, A. C. (2012). *Teaming: How organizations learn, innovate, and compete in the knowledge economy.* Jossey-Bass.

Senge, P. M. (1990). *The fifth discipline: The art and practice of the learning organization.* Doubleday.

Dweck, C. S. (2006). *Mindset: The new psychology of success.* Random House.

Smerek, R. (2017). *Organizational learning and performance: The science and practice of building a learning culture.* Oxford University Press.

The Clarity Discipline

Bossidy, L., & Charan, R. (2002). *Execution: The discipline of getting things done.* Crown Business.

Frankl, V. E. (2006). *Man's search for meaning.* Beacon Press. (Original work published 1946).

Heath, C., & Heath, D. (2013). *Decisive: How to make better decisions in life and work.* Crown Business.

Kahneman, D., & Tversky, A. (1979). "Prospect theory: An analysis of decision under risk." *Econometrica, 47*(2), 263–291.

Raue, S., Tang, S. H., Weiland, C., & Wenzlik, C. (2013). The GRPI model–an approach for team development. White Paper Draft, SE Group.

The Safety Discipline

Edmondson, A. C. (2012). *Teaming: How organizations learn, innovate, and compete in the knowledge economy.* Jossey-Bass.

Goleman, D. (1995). *Emotional intelligence: Why it can matter more than IQ.* Bantam Books.

Gallup Workplace Research. (2018). *The power of recognition in driving engagement.*

The Connection Discipline

Holt-Lunstad, J., Smith, T. B., & Layton, J. B. (2010). "Social relationships and mortality risk: A meta-analytic review." *PLoS Medicine, 7*(7), Article e1000316.

Murthy, V. H. (2017). *Work and the loneliness epidemic.* Harvard Business Review. Available at https://hbr.org/2017/09/work-and-the-loneliness-epidemic (accessed April 18, 2025).

Pink, D. H. (2009). *Drive: The surprising truth about what motivates us.* Riverhead Books.

Coyle, D. (2018). *The culture code: The secrets of highly successful groups.* Bantam Books.

Grover, S., & Furnham, A. (2023). "Coaching culture: An evidence review and framework for future research and practice." *International Coaching Psychology Review, 18*(2), 123–140.

The Action Discipline

Charan, R., Drotter, S., & Noel, J. (2011). *The leadership pipeline: How to build the leadership-powered company.* Jossey-Bass.

Collins, J. (2001). *Good to great: Why some companies make the leap… and others don't.* Harper Business.

Johnson, B. (1996). *Polarity management: Identifying and managing unsolvable problems.* HRD Press.

The Adaptability Discipline

Collins, J., & Hansen, M. T. (2011). *Great by choice: Uncertainty, chaos, and luck—why some thrive despite them all.* Harper Business.

Csikszentmihalyi, M. (1990). *Flow: The psychology of optimal experience.* Harper & Row.

Rock, D., & Grant, H. (2016). Why diverse teams are smarter. *Harvard Business Review, 4*(4), 2–5.

The Celebration Discipline

Gallup. (2022, March 30). *Playing favorites in employee recognition? Here's how to get it right.* Gallup.

Gallup. (2024). *State of the global workplace: 2024 Report.* Gallup Press.

Tuckman, B. W. (1965). "Developmental sequence in small groups." *Psychological Bulletin, 63*(6), 384–399.

The 7 Disciplines of an Effective Team

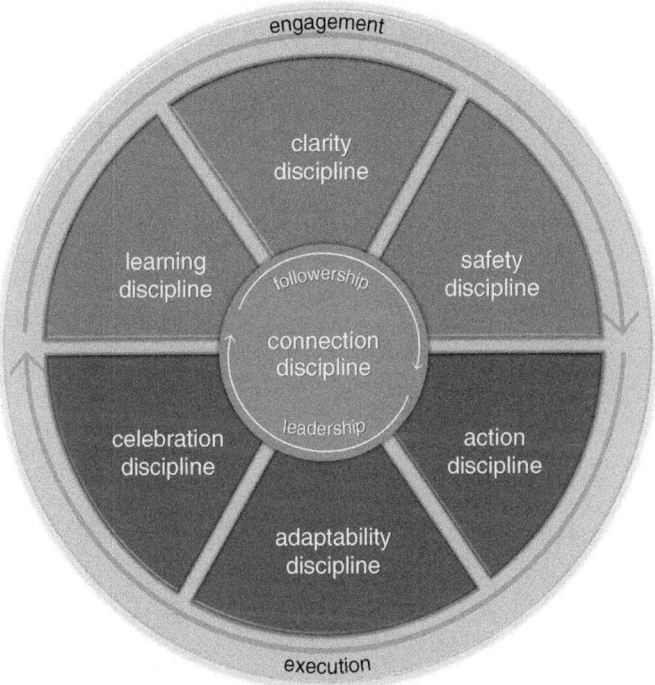

Index

A

acknowledgement, 121, 124

Action Discipline

about, 97–98,
134–136, 147

applying, 109–112

avoiding priority
traps, 106

both/and
thinking, 103–105

decisive
decisions, 99–100

follower effect, 113

foundation of
execution, 98–99

polarity
paradox, 100–103

resources for, 145

team engagement, 105

Thomas's journal
recap, 112–113

understanding priority
traps, 106–109

acts of kindness,
collaborating and,
79

Adaptability Discipline

about, 115, 136–137, 147

feedback loops,
115–116

resources for, 146

situational awareness,
115

strategic flexibility,
116–118

Thomas's journal
recap, 118–119

air we breathe, 60–61

Argyris, C. (author), 143

awareness, team
engagement
and, 105

B

barriers, to Learning
  Discipline, 36–37
Bossidy, L. (author), 144
both/and thinking,
  103–105, 110
Bridwell, Tony A. (author),
  1–2, 3, 143

C

Campbell, J. (author), 143
Celebration Discipline
  about, 121, 139–141, 147
  acknowledgement, 121
  execution in action,
    122–123
  follower effect, 124
  reflection, 121–122
  renewal, 122
  resources for, 146
  Thomas's journal recap,
    123–124
change, inevitability
  of, 116
character, as a seed of trust,
  63, 132–133
Charan, R. (author),
  144, 145
Clarity Discipline

about, 43–44,
  131–132, 147
clarity in action, 50–52
follower effect, 55
how to achieve clarity,
  48–49
Leah on, 53
resources for, 144
team struggles with
  clarity, 47–48
Thomas's journal
  recap, 53–54
what it is, 44–47
coaches, 74, 80–83
"Coaching Culture" (Coyle
  and Furnham), 145
co-creation, clarity as, 132
collaboration, fostering, 95
collaborators, 74–80
Collins, J. (author), 145, 146
compassion, as a seed of
  trust, 63, 132–133
competence, as a seed of
  trust, 63, 132–133
Connection Discipline
  about, 71–73,
    133–134, 147
  building connections,
    92–93

coaches, 80–83
collaborators, 74–77
components of, 73–91
counselors, 83–91
follower effect, 95
remote workers, 78–80
resources for, 145
Thomas's journal
recap, 94–95
connections, 69, 72,
92–93
consistency, as a seed of
trust, 63, 132–133
contributions,
acknowledging, 124
counselors, 74, 83–91
Coyle, D. (author), 145
creating shared moments,
133–134
Csikszentmihalyi, M.
(author), 146
The Culture Code
(Coyle), 145

D
decision framing, 113
decision-making,
decisive, 99–100,
113, 134–136

decisive decisions, 99–100,
113, 134–136
Decisive (Heath and
Heath), 144
"Developmental Sequence
in Small Groups"
(Tuckman), 146
disciplines, 22–25, 98.
See also specific
disciplines
The Do Over (Bridwell), 143
double-loop
mindset, 34, 27–40
doubt, 127–130
Drive (Pink), 145
Drotter, S. (author), 145
Dweck, C. S. (author), 144

E
Edmondson, A. C.
(author), 144
Emotional Intelligence
(Goleman), 144
emotional safety, 61
empathy, collaborating
and, 79
execution
in action, 122–123
aligned, 110

execution (*continued*)
  disciplines of, 98
  foundation of, 98–99
Execution (Bossidy and
    Charan), 144
expectations, aligning,
    131–132

F
faith
  about, 59, 63
  building with, 132–133
  Leah on, 126–127
  role of in trust, 67–68
feedback loops,
    115–116, 119
The Fifth Discipline
    (Senge), 144
flexibility, strategic, 116–118
Flow (Csikszentmihalyi), 146
follower effect, 41, 55, 69,
    95, 113, 119, 124
followership
  key lessons on, 41, 55,
    69, 95, 113, 119, 124
  redefining, 30–32
The Follower Effect
    (Bridwell), 1–2, 143
Forgiveness, 89–91, 95

fostering collaboration, 95
fulfillment quotation, 73
Furnham, A. (author), 145

G
Gallup Workplace Research,
    145
giving back, 79–80
Goleman, D. (author), 144
Good to Great (Collins),
    145
grace, collaborating
    and, 79
Grant, H., 146
Great by Choice (Collins
    and Hansen), 146
Grover, S. (author), 145

H
Hansen, M. T.
    (author), 146
Heath, C (author), 144
Heath, D.
    (author), 144
Hemingway, Ernest
    (writer), 1, 2
*The Hero with a
    Thousand Faces*
    (Campbell), 143

Holt-Lunstad, J.
(author), 145
hybrid teams, 78–80
hyperconnectivity
paradox, 86

I
isolationism, combating,
87–89

J
Johnson, B. (author), 145

K
Kahneman, D. (author),
36–37, 144

L
Layton, J. B. (author), 145
leadership
about, 76–77
key lessons on, 41, 55, 69,
95, 113, 119, 124
redefining, 30–32
The Leadership Pipeline
(Charan, Drotter and
Noel), 145
Learning Discipline
about, 27–30, 131, 147

barriers to, 36–37
follower effect, 41
redefining leadership
and followership,
30–32
resources for, 143–144
starting point, 32–36
Thomas's breakthrough,
37–39
Thomas's journal
recap, 39–40
learn-unlearn-relearn, 116
listening, starting by, 131

M
Mindset (Dweck), 144
model vulnerability, 94
modeling safety, 69
momentum, sustained,
111–113, 123
Murthy, V. H. (author), 145

N
Noel. J. (author), 145

O
*Organizational Learning
and Performance*
(Smerek), 144

overemphasizing, risks
of, 104
over-indexing, risks of, 104

P

perfectionism, 104
physical safety, 61
Pink, D. H. (author), 145
pivot strategically, 119
*Playing Favorites
in Employee
Recognition? Here's
How to Get it Right*
(Gallup), 146
Polarity Management
(Johnson), 145
polarity paradox,
100–103
*The Power of Recognition
in Driving
Engagement*
(Gallup Workplace
Research), 145
priority fixation, 106
priority trap, 106–109
proactive adaptability,
leveraging, 119
progress, reflecting on, 124

"Prospect Theory"
(Kahneman and
Tversky), 144
psychological safety,
59, 60–61, 81

Q

quality, 73, 104

R

Raue, S. (author), 144
recharging, 124
reflecting on progress, 124
reflection, 27–40, 121–122
reinforcing connection, 69
remote workers, 78–80
renewal, 122
resources, 143–147
Rock, D. (author), 146
Rule of 2
Degrees, 45–46, 53

S

safety, modeling, 69
Safety Discipline
about, 57–60,
132–133, 147
air we breathe, 60–61

follower effect, 69

four seeds of trust, 62–64

overcoming

weeds, 64–66

recognizing and

addressing

weeds, 66–67

resources for, 144–145

role of faith in trust, 67–68

Thomas's journal

recap, 68–69

Saturday Morning Tea

(Bridwell), 1, 3, 143

scaffold connection, 73, 94

Schön, D. A. (author), 143

self-efficacy, 81

Senge, P. M. (author), 144

shared moments,

creating, 133–134

situational awareness, 115

Smerek, R. (author), 144

Smith, T. B. (author), 145

social connection, 73

"Social Relationships and

Mortality Risk"

(Holt-Lunstad,

Smith and

Layton), 145

starting point, for Learning

Discipline, 32–36

State of the global

workplace: 2024

Report (Gallup), 146

strategic flexibility,

116–118

strategic pivots, 119

structure, social

connection and, 73

sustained momentum,

111–113, 123

T

Tang, S. H., 144

Teaming (Edmondson), 144

teams

about, 2–4

engagement in, 105

processes in Learning

Discipline, 27–40

struggles with

clarity, 47–48

tension, in teams, 109

Theory in Practice (Argyris

and Schön), 143

thinking, both/and,

103–105, 110

trust
 about, 59–60
 broken, 64–66
 building with, 132–133
 cultivating, 69
 four seeds of, 62–64,
  132–133
 Leah on, 126–127
 role of faith in, 67–68
Tuckman, B. W.
  (author), 146
Tversky, A. (author),
  36–37, 144

V
Vogler, C. (author), 143
vulnerability, building
  with, 132–133

W
Weiland, C., 144
Wenzlik, C., 144
*Work and the Loneliness
 Epidemic*
  (Murthy), 145
The Writer's Journey
  (Vogler), 143